THE WAR
IN PICTURES
FIFTH YEAR

———— ⸻ ————

ODHAMS PRESS LIMITED
LONG ACRE. LONDON, W. C. 2

ALLIES LAND IN NORMANDY
Activity on the beaches as vehicles and supplies
are unloaded from huge landing craft offshore.

THE YEAR OF LIBERATION

I N the fifth year of the struggle against Nazi Germany, the enemy, until so recently the master of Europe, found himself on the defensive for the first time. The United Nations were now in a position to demonstrate their overwhelming superiority in strength on land, at sea and in the air. Both on the Russian front and in North Africa the German armies had suffered great and decisive defeats. In Europe itself—where the final blow was now eagerly awaited—the Nazi oppressors were finding it increasingly difficult and costly to quell the rising spirit of the patriot forces and underground movements in every country under their yoke.

During the previous two years secret preparations had been going forward on a tremendous scale for the promised Anglo-American offensive against Hitler's "Fortress of Europe." In a series of important conferences held in Washington, Casablanca, Moscow and elsewhere, the leaders of Britain, the U.S.A. and the Soviet Union, together with their military advisers, planned what have since proved to be the most gigantic operations in the history of warfare. They planned these operations down to the last detail.

The results of those long months of careful preparation, in which the British Prime Minister was the leading spirit, began to take shape with the landings in Sicily on 10 July, 1943. This virtually marked the opening of an all-powerful and continued offensive which was to liberate one oppressed country of Europe after another and bring the Allied armies right up to the gates of Germany itself in little more than twelve months. To a future historian, one of the most remarkable aspects of this period of the war now under review will be the degree of co-operation achieved by the United Nations. As the months went by, the value of the combined effort became clearly evident by the way in which the attacks launched from the south, east and west were perfectly dovetailed into the mighty plan that was gradually unfolding. Never had such unity and strength of purpose been forged between nations for the overthrow of a common enemy.

The prelude to the battles for the liberation of Europe was the total defeat and annihilation of

FLORENCE SET FREE. The first troops to enter Florence were South Africans of the Eighth Army. In order to delay Allied progress to the heart of the city, the Germans had blown up five of the six bridges spanning the river Arno, leaving only the famous fourteenth-century Ponte Vecchio. (A view of the historic structure appears on page 213.) Even that was blocked at either end by enemy demolitions. The picture above shows civilians crowding around British vehicles halted in a street while on their way through the oldest part of Florence.

the Axis armies in North Africa. The spring of 1943 saw the victorious end of the North African campaign with the fall of Tunis and Bizerta and the capture of over one quarter of a million prisoners. Meanwhile, on the Eastern front, the way into Europe was opened up through the elimination of the Nazi hordes on and beyond the River Don following the immortal three-months' defence of Stalingrad. Both at Stalingrad and at El Alamein, the enemy's advance was at last checked and turned into non-stop retreat.

INVASION OF ITALY

The occupation of Sicily was completed within six weeks. It was a remarkable campaign fought amid most difficult country. By the occupation of this, the largest of the Mediterranean islands, the last serious obstacle to Allied shipping in the western part of that sea was removed and the enemy had lost an important group of key air bases. Before the end of the fighting in Sicily, moreover, the Italian dictator, faced by the growing revolt of his people, found himself in an embarrassing situation. After a special meeting of the Fascist Grand Council in Rome on 24 July, Mussolini was forced to resign. The first of the fascist dictators had fallen.

Immediately after the victory in Sicily the Allied forces crossed the Messina Straits into Italy itself, where the initial objectives in the " toe " were quickly gained with little opposition from the enemy. Thus, on the fourth anniversary of the outbreak of war, a first foothold was regained on the mainland of Europe, and the British Navy again held complete mastery in the Mediterranean.

The opening phase of the invasion of Europe was timed to coincide with new and far-reaching advances by the Red Army in the East. From the neighbourhood of Smolensk right down to the Donetz in the south, mighty Russian forces were pushing back the enemy relentlessly, inflicting upon him unparalleled losses in men and material. The outstandingly successful summer campaign by the Red Army, culminating in the recapture of the city of Kharkov on 23 August, made way for the liberation of the Ukraine, by far the most valuable part of Russian territory then left in German hands. Everywhere in Russia the enemy was beating a hasty retreat, and a costly one.

On the same day that the Allies landed in Italy an armistice was signed by that country agreeing to the unconditional surrender of all her armed forces. This, however, was not made known until 8 September. It meant that the whole of Italy's territory and her military and industrial power were at the disposal of the United Nations for the prosecution of the war against Germany.

Almost a week after the initial landings on the " toe " of Italy, the Fifth Army (composed mainly of Americans, but including several British divisions) made new assaults on the beaches at Salerno, south of Naples. Here, however, the Allies met with some serious opposition, for the Germans had meanwhile had time to concentrate very considerable forces in this limited area, where the hills, rising steeply from the shore, afforded them excellent defensive positions. For several days the situation at Salerno was critical, during which time the enemy made wildly extravagant claims that the Allied forces were on the point of being pushed back into the sea. But by 15 September the critical stage of the battle was at last over and the Allied beachhead was firmly established. Though the landings at Salerno were well worth while, and achieved their object, they were made at considerable risk at the extreme range of air cover. They proved that strong air cover is always essential for such operations.

Meanwhile, progress was made northwards on the Adriatic side of Italy by the Eighth Army, which had occupied the important harbours of Taranto and Brindisi. On 1 October the Fifth Army entered Naples, the largest city and seaport to be taken so far on the Italian mainland. Although the Germans had destroyed the harbour as far as possible before retreating from the city, British and American engineers worked swiftly to make it usable again. Thirteen days later the Badoglio Government declared war against Germany, and Italy thereby became a co-belligerent of the United Nations.

ADVANCE TO THE VOLTURNO

From early October, however, the campaign in Italy, which in its initial stages had moved along fairly rapidly, was considerably slowed down. This was due not only to stiffening resistance by the enemy but also to the difficulties caused by the mountain country and the bad weather. Winter had arrived much earlier than is usual in Italy. Consequently, the use of our tactical air power was, for a time, greatly handicapped. Nevertheless, the Fifth Army advanced to the line of the Volturno, where they established a bridgehead on 7 October, and fierce fighting went

GERMAN AIRCRAFT FACTORY WRECKED. Apparently secure in the belief that East Prussia was beyond the range of daylight bombers, German defences were taken by surprise on 9 October, 1943, when strong formations of "Flying Fortresses" from Britain attacked the huge Focke-Wulf aircraft factory at Marienburg, south-east of Danzig. This target lay some 200 miles beyond Berlin and the flight involved a 1,800-miles round

trip from base, the bombers being in the air for about ten hours. This plant, which was virtually destroyed by the blow, was believed to have assembled about half of all Germany's "F.W. 190" fighter planes. Many new aircraft parked outside the works were also smashed. The picture on these pages shows dense smoke and flame rising from the wrecked factory as some of the "Fortresses" leave the target for the long flight back to Britain.

on here for many days in appalling weather conditions. Meanwhile, the Eighth Army reached the Sangro River and by mid-November had established a firm bridgehead beyond it.

Despite the fact that the advance in Italy had been painfully slow and that by the end of December, 1943, the way leading to the prize of Rome was still closed to our armies, the campaign had achieved certain important results. These were really of immense value, even though they were not to be measured in terms of miles. It had forced Italy to give up the war on the side of Germany. It had already gained for the Allies a number of useful airfields in southern Italy from which to operate against the Germans in south-eastern Europe. Moreover, it had done much to achieve the wider dispersal of the enemy's strength by forcing him to concentrate large forces of his troops in Italy. This was very important in the strategy of the United Nations.

While the Allies continued to be hampered by the hard mountain country and the weather, the Germans took advantage of the situation to keep the front more or less static in order to save troops and build up their reserves for defensive battles farther north. On one side of Italy the Fifth Army was battling hard against the Germans entrenched in the area of the Garigliano River, while on the other the Eighth Army was thrusting slowly, mile by mile towards Pescara, having established a bridgehead across the Moro River. By the beginning of January both the Fifth and Eighth Armies were wresting more territory from the Germans in their struggle for possession of the roads to Rome, but limited advances were made under difficult conditions.

LANDINGS AT ANZIO

On 22 January there was a new development in the Italian campaign with the Allied landing in strength on the west coast near Anzio, some thirty miles south of Rome. While it was popularly thought that this event would lead to the early capture of Rome, such high ambitions were never in the minds of those who planned the difficult operation. The problem of supply was a very real one, and in this respect the Germans had a great advantage. For while the enemy had the roads and railways in his rear, the Allied troops had to rely entirely on supplies by sea. The real object of the landing was, in fact, to extend the Allied front and therefore to compel the Germans to bring up more troops for their own defence. Although there was no spectacular

advance inland, the Allied strategy of the following months was to build up the relatively narrow bridgehead into a solid front which would be able to withstand the very heavy counter-attacks which the Germans launched against it. It succeeded. For the enemy was forced, against his will, to use up many divisions he could ill afford in unsuccessful attempts to smash the bridgehead.

BATTLES ROUND CASSINO

Meanwhile very heavy and bitter fighting was taking place on the main Fifth Army front, particularly around Cassino. Here the enemy was pinned down in some strength, and such small gains as he won were made only at heavy cost. This concentration of the enemy's strength on the Central Italian front was to serve the Allies better than was thought at the time. The German commander, von Kesselring, was now obliged to draw on reserve troops from north Italy, France, the Balkans and elsewhere. So, although the fighting in Italy during the early months of 1944 was more or less static, the Allies were certainly not on the losing side.

During the months preceding the opening of the so-called "Second Front" from the west, the British and American air forces carried out an unprecedented offensive against targets in Germany and the occupied territories of north-west Europe. From the winter onwards these day and night attacks were continued almost incessantly, growing in intensity all the time. Particular attention was given to secret military targets along the coast of Northern France and in the country immediately behind it. Allied bombers and fighter bombers were gradually reducing the vital German defences of the "West Wall," thereby preparing the way for the invading land forces. This aerial offensive was an essential part of the great Allied plan for the liberation of Europe. The work of the air crews was magnificently done and saved thousands of lives when the invasion began.

A new stage in the air war against Germany, begun in January, was the development of the two-way offensive from the west and the south, from Allied bases both in Britain and Italy. This meant that for the first time no part of Germany or of her satellite states in the Balkans was beyond the reach of these bombers. Every German war factory was now to feel the blows of the powerful Anglo-American air combination. Thousand-plane raids on specific industrial targets in the Reich, such as that made by Bomber Command on Schweinfurt on the night of 24 February, were becoming increasingly common. Berlin had its heaviest raid ot the war exactly a month later (24 March) when over 1,000 bombers dropped 2,500 tons of high explosive and incendiary bombs on the German capital.

Meanwhile, on the Eastern front, the Red Army continued to make remarkable progress the Ukrainian capital no fewer than twelve German divisions were routed: more than 15,000 of the enemy were killed and some 6,000 taken prisoner. Such was the importance of this victory that it was hailed in Moscow with the biggest salute of guns of the war to that time.

By the New Year the Red Army had recaptured many more keypoints all along the front,

GERMAN PRISONERS IN THE WEST. The Allied landings in Normandy added seriously to Germany's manpower problem. During the firs: two months after "D-Day" well over 100,000 prisoners were captured as well as great quantities of enemy equipment and war material. These severe .osses led to the enemy's swift re'reat across Northern France and the Belgian border. The picture above shows a great column of German prisoners, captured in the woods north of Amiens, being marched through a French town with British and "Maquis" in charge.

following the final liberation of Kharkov in the summer of 1943. Keeping up their mighty offensive along almost the whole length of the front, the Russians cleared the enemy from the Donetz Basin, recapturing such important cities as Taganrog, Stalino, Zaporozhe and Melitopol: farther north they regained possession of Bryansk, Smolensk, Vitebsk and Nevel, all vital communications centres. One of the greatest Russian victories during their autumn offensive was the recapture, on 6 November, of the big industrial city of Kiev, third largest city of the Soviet Union. During the course of extremely bitter fighting for and much territory had been cleared of the enemy. Desperate German counter-attacks, particularly against Kiev, had been spent, and the battered enemy divisions were in no position to check the coming blows from the Red Army. The Russian policy of forcing the German commanders to use up their rapidly dwindling reserves was being carried out in a ruthless manner: it was to be continued in the months ahead.

On 5 January the Red Army broadened out its front in the Kiev salient by taking Byelaya-Tserkov and Berdichev, two of the northern strong-points held by the enemy in the Dnieper

MOSCOW SALUTES THE RED ARMY. During a year which brought the most tremendous series of victories to he Red Army, fighting on a front of more than one thousand miles, the guns of the Russian capital roared out many salutes in its honour. The photograph reproduced on these pages gives a striking impression of the centre of Moscow on the night following the recapture of Kiev, capital of the Ukraine and third largest city of the Soviet Union, on 6 November, 1943. This important event marked the climax of the Red Army's autumn

offensive and was celebrated with great rejoicing in towns and villages throughout the Soviet Union. In Moscow twenty-four salvos were fired from 324 guns (the biggest salute of the war up to that date) and there were also magnificent displays of rockets, flares and coloured lights. Kiev was held by the Germans for more than two years, being captured in September, 1941, three months after the invasion of the U.S.S.R. By the liberation of Kiev, no obstacles were left between the advancing Red Army and the frontier of Poland, 120 miles distant.

Bend, and their troops began to cross the 1939 frontier of Poland. Two days later advanced Russian units had captured a town fifteen miles on the Polish side, and by 12 January the key junction of Sarny, on the Kiev-Warsaw railway, had been taken. Good progress was also made along the front farther south where the big town of Kirovograd was surrounded. Other regions

February and altogether nine German infantry divisions and one tank division—comprising 100,000 to 120,000 men—were encircled. This was the biggest operation of its kind since von Paulus's Sixth Army of 330,000 men was wiped out or captured at Stalingrad a year earlier.

Meanwhile, on 18 January, the Russian High Command announced new offensives at the

FIGHTING IN A PACIFIC JUNGLE. Very heavy fighting occurred on Bougainville Island, in the Northern Solomons, during March, 1944, when Japanese forces launched an attack against the beachhead established on Empress Augusta Bay by the Americans. The enemy attack failed, however, and the Allied beachhead was re-established and expanded after more than 1,000 Japanese had been killed. The picture shows U.S. infantrymen, their bayonets fixed, crouching behind a tank during an advance against the Japanese on Bougainville.

held by the Germans there were isolated, and Red Army forces actually reached the River Bug. This meant that the railway line running down from Lvov to Odessa—a communications link of the most vital importance to the enemy—was now gravely threatened.

The Red Army's advance south and southwest of Kiev towards the Lvov-Odessa railway proved a disaster of some magnitude for the enemy divisions still left in the Dnieper Bend between Kanyev and Smyela. Two great Russian forces thrusting from the east and the west linked up near Zvenigorodka in the early days of

northern end of their front. On the Leningrad front the Red Army broke through the strongly fortified defences which the enemy had constructed over a long period. The advance was very successful: on the next day the Leningrad-Novgorod railway was cut and on 20 January Novgorod itself was captured.

By 24-25 January the Russian armies were advancing steadily on a front of fifty miles in the Leningrad region. By the liquidation of the German beachhead south-west of the city they gained control of a continuous stretch along the southern shore of the Gulf of Finland more than fifty miles in length. This allowed the Soviet Baltic Fleet to sail again and put ashore supplies for the Red Army. The swift advances of the Red Army in the far north led to peace moves by the Finnish Government. The terms offered for an armistice by the Soviet Union in April, however, were rejected despite appeals from Sweden and the U.S.A. to Finland to accept them.

FAR EAST ADVANCES

While the interest in the war was focused mainly on Europe during the past year, the vast campaign against the Japanese in the Far East was going ahead steadily. Ever since May, 1942, Japan had been on the defensive on three of the main four fronts. Only on the China front were the Japanese still attacking in the various areas they held in that country, but such thrusts as they could periodically make were on a limited scale. All the time the guerrilla forces of General Chiang Kai-shek and the Chinese Red Army were in action against them.

Elsewhere in the Far East very noteworthy gains were made from September, 1943, and by land, sea and air the United Nations gradually drew the ring tighter around Japan. Hard fighting continued in New Guinea during the summer and in mid-September the Australians in a series of bold landings, captured the important bases of Salamaua and Lae. On 1 November American Marines landed on Bougainville, the most northerly of the Solomon Islands. Here the Japanese counter-attacked with heavy reinforcements, but after severe fighting they were repulsed.

The campaign in the South Pacific, resulting chiefly in the recapture of the Solomons, New Georgia and most of New Guinea, removed the threat—at one time a very grave one—to Australia, one of the main Allied bases in the war against Japan. The decisive blows which saved Australia were staged at Milne Bay (August, 1943), where the Japanese sustained their first great defeat on land, and on Guadalcanal in the Solomons. These two important events, which may be paralleled with El Alamein and Stalingrad in the European conflict, turned the tide in the Far East and gave the United Nations the initiative.

In the Central Pacific, 1,000 miles north of the Solomons, a major attack was launched in the Gilbert Islands by U.S. Marines in November, 1943. It was a swift but extremely ferocious campaign, the main atolls of Tarawa (with its vital airfield on Betio Island) and Makin being recaptured. This was followed in February by successful land attacks on the Marshall Islands, and in March and April by heavy air blows against the Admiralty Islands and the important Japanese naval base at Truk. By the summer the war was reaching ever closer to Japan with heavy air and naval attacks on such island groups as the Carolines, the Bonins, the Kuriles and the Marianas. In the last group, the key island of Saipan fell to the Americans in July. Altogether more than 400,000 Japanese have been killed in the Pacific area alone.

No less important was the Burma front, where British, Indian and American-led Chinese troops were fighting a difficult campaign amid some of the toughest jungle and mountain country in the world. In 1942 the Japanese forces advanced up through Burma until they were halted on the Assam border. The Burma campaign on four fronts in 1943-1944 aimed at re-establishing land communications between India and China by the re-opening of the New Burma Road. Much of the success that was achieved was due to the development of Allied air power in Burma—we had complete air superiority—and the remarkable exploits of the " Chindits," a great wrecking expedition led by the late Brigadier Wingate, D.S.O., which operated for more than three months in the difficult jungle country of Central Burma well behind the enemy's lines.

" D-DAY "

On 6 June, two days after General Alexander's troops captured Rome, the Allies launched their long-expected assault from the West. Following weeks of intensive bombing and ceaseless strafing of enemy defence positions and troops and communications over north-west Europe by the British and U.S. Air Forces, a powerful amphibious attack was begun on the coast of Normandy to the west of Caen. A notable feature of the initial operations was the use of airborne forces which was on the greatest scale up to that date. These airborne forces, dropped at vital key points behind the coast, preceded the land troops arriving by sea. By the second day all the landing beaches had been cleared of the enemy, the town of Bayeux had been captured and fighting was going on in the suburbs of Caen. At the end of the first week the Anglo-American armies held a stretch of fifty miles of the Normandy coastline from Quineville in the west to the mouth of the river Orne. All this was achieved despite the fact that the Allies had no big port and all their supplies had to be landed on the open beaches.

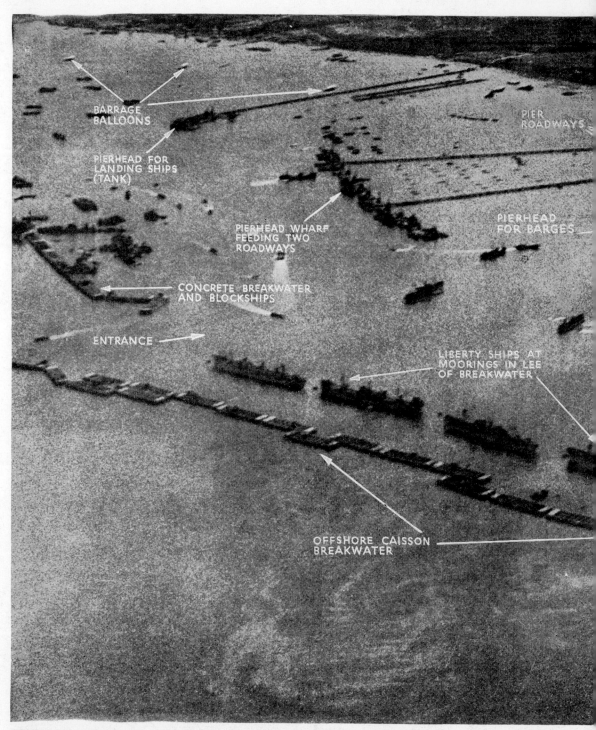

READY-MADE HARBOUR CROSSES THE CHANNEL. One of the best kept secrets of the landings in Normandy in June, 1944, was the use of a remarkable prefabricated harbour. This ready-made port, as large as Gibraltar, was towed across the Channel in sections and placed down off the barren coast of the Arromanches beaches. The port, with its huge concrete breakwaters, steel caissons, piers, old ships and so on, comprised over 1,500,000 tons and was two miles in length and one mile wide. It achieved a complete strategic and tactical surprise to

NORMANDY

BARRAGE
BALLOONS

FLOATING
DERRICK

DISPERSED
SHIPPING

INSHORE BREAKWATER
OF CONCRETE
CAISSONS

ENTRANCE

the Germans who had believed, not unnaturally, that no landings in France could possibly be secured by the Allied invasion forces without a port. In fact, the prefabricated harbour enabled a force of more than 250,000 men to land on an inhospitable part of the Normandy coastline. It was surely one of the most imaginative pieces of engineering in the history of the war, and one that has revolutionized amphibious warfare. The photograph above gives a general view of the prefabricated port in position showing the outer breakwaters and inside piers

GENERAL DE GAULLE RETURNS TO PARIS. On the day following the liberation of Paris, the acknowledged leader of France headed a great procession from the Arc de Triomphe through the main streets of the capital to the Cathedral of Notre Dame. Here a solemn thanksgiving service was held. As the General arrived at the cathedral an attempt was made on his life by snipers hidden in an adjoining building, but their bullets fortunately missed him. The picture above shows General de Gaulle leaving Notre Dame after the service of thanksgiving.

While the British were advancing in the region of Caen and southwards to Caumont and Tilly, where there was heavy and prolonged fighting, the Americans swept across the Cotentin peninsula to the Gulf of St. Malo. Their object, of course, was to isolate Cherbourg and capture the port from the rear. On 29 June Cherbourg fell and the whole peninsula was firmly in Allied hands. Thus the bridgehead in Normandy was made quite secure and the first stage in the liberation of France was completed.

The next stage of the fighting in Normandy was one of slow progress all along the line as the Germans launched their expected counter-attacks. Such advances as there were, were achieved only by close and bitter fighting. The capture of Caen on 8 July, however, marked an important gain on the British-Canadian sector of the front for it gave us solid bridgeheads over the rivers Odon and Orne. Fighting was extremely severe here because the enemy had concentrated picked infantry and armoured forces—some of them switched from the Russian front—to stem the Allied advance into the open country. Once an Allied break-through was achieved, as the Germans knew well, it would have consequences that would be far-reaching.

By the beginning of August this break-through was achieved. The battle became one of movement with the Allies holding the initiative everywhere. The Americans advanced rapidly to St. Malo and southwards to the Loire, cutting off the whole of the Brittany peninsula and the Germans contained there. Driving westwards they liberated great areas of Western France, reaching Chartres and Orleans by the middle of the month. A determined enemy counter-attack from the region of Mortain, which attempted to split the Allied armies in two, was successfully held. Meanwhile, by the Canadian and British thrust southwards from Caen towards Falaise, and by the turn of the columns from the south to Argentan, a large part of the German forces was trapped in the Falaise " pocket." The enemy was now in full flight towards the Seine, constantly attacked both from the air and on the ground.

On 15 August a second Allied invasion of France was made along the Riviera coast. Only light enemy resistance was met with, however, and rapid advances were made to Grenoble and up the Rhone Valley. As in Normandy and Brittany, great assistance was given to the Anglo-American forces by the redoubtable men of the " Maquis." They themselves liberated almost the entire area between the Loire and the Pyrenees.

During the last days of August the Allied progress across France was still more remarkable. On 25 August Paris itself was liberated by the " Maquis " and an armoured division under General Leclerc. The Americans pressed on eastwards and crossed the River Marne at several points, capturing the towns of Rheims and Laon on the last day of the month. By 1 September General Patton's troops had crossed the Meuse

and entered the historic town of Verdun, reaching a point only thirty miles from the German frontier. The British and Canadians, meanwhile, had begun a series of remarkable advances from their bridgeheads over the Seine below Paris. In two days, 30-31 August, an advance of sixty miles took the British to the far bank of the Somme at Amiens. Next day the British drove on another thirty miles to take Arras, while the Canadians took the port of Dieppe. On 3 September, in one of the most rapid advances in military history, the British Second Army raced across the Belgian frontier and in the evening entered the city of Brussels, which had been under Nazi occupation for over four years.

Thus, at the close of the fifth year of the Second World War, the liberating forces of the United Nations, pressing with growing tempo from the east and the west, had driven the German aggressors almost back to their own frontiers.

LIBERATION OF BRUSSELS. After more than four years of suffering under German rule, the people of Brussels went wild with joy on the day that British and Belgian troops re-entered the city. Lining the main streets of the capital, the cheering crowds waved flags and threw flowers into the Allied vehicles as they passed by. The picture shows a street in liberated Brussels with young Belgian girls riding on one of the Allied cars.

ALLIES LAND IN ITALY

3 SEPTEMBER, 1943

On 3 September, 1943, a special announcement from General Eisenhower's headquarters gave news of the first Allied landings on the Italian mainland. The whole world acclaimed the initial attack on the continent of Europe. Landings followed a terrific artillery barrage from our batteries across the Straits of Messina, which effectively silenced enemy guns on the Calabrian coast. Weeks of devastating air attacks, designed to neutralize the enemy's airfields and to disorganize his communications, contributed much to the success of the landings. Zero hour was 4.30 a.m., when a huge fleet of invasion barges and landing craft appeared off the Italian coast and British and Canadian troops of the Eighth went ashore under a continuous "air umbrella" provided by the R.A.F. Landings were made at many places on the toe of Italy between Reggio and San Giovanni and the Eighth Army pushed inland rapidly, meeting negligible opposition. Before dusk on the same day Reggio and its important airfield, San Giovanni, and a number of other places were captured. Shortly before the invasion General Montgomery, in a message to his troops, said: "To the Eighth Army is given the great honour of being the first troops of the Allied armies to land on the mainland of the continent of Europe. We have a good plan and air support on a greater scale than we have ever had before. There can only be one end to this next battle—another success. Forward to victory. Let us knock Italy out of the war." The picture shows General Montgomery saluting his troops from a Bren carrier in Reggio.

ITALY SURRENDERS UNCONDITIONALLY

The same day as the Allies began their invasion, Italy signed an armistice agreeing to the unconditional surrender of all her armed forces. This news, however, was kept a secret until 8 September. Shortly afterwards Marshal Badoglio broadcast a message to the Italian people, in which he stated: "The Italian forces will cease all acts of hostilities against the Anglo-American forces. They will, however, oppose attacks of any other forces." Meanwhile British and Canadian troops continued to widen their hold on the Calabrian coastline and to advance several miles farther inland. Only at Bagnara was stiff resistance encountered, but here the Germans were overcome after hard fighting. On 6 September the Eighth Army captured Palmi and San Stefano, and next day advanced another twelve miles to occupy Rosarno. The pictures on these pages show: top left, part of the Allied invasion fleet; bottom left, widespread havoc caused to Italian railways near Reggio by R.A.F. bombing; bottom right, amphibious "ducks" of the Eighth Army going ashore on the southern coast of Italy.

ALLIED BOMBERS HIT ITALIAN INDUSTRIES

On 2 September Allied bombers, based on Sicily, made a 1,200 mile flight to attack industrial targets in Northern Italy. Bolzano and Trento, at the entrance to the Brenner Pass (through which all direct traffic from Germany to Italy must pass), were heavily bombed. At Trento, both rail and road bridges over the River Adige were destroyed. The railways were b'ocked by landslides caused by high-explosive bombs. At Bologna and Cance'lo huge fires were started among railway yards and warehouses. In a broadcast to the Italian people, Marshal Badoglio said: "Italy's industries are paralysed. Her communications, which are so important because of the geographic formation of the country, are thrown nto confusion. Her supplies are completely exhausted. There is not a single point in the national territory which is not open to enemy attack without adequate defence. In these circumstances the Italian Government can no longer bear the responsibility for continu'ng a war which has already cost Italy the destruction of her towns; the annihilation of her industries." The Germans considered it so important that all industries should continue that all towns were placed under complete German control and all factories run under German supervision. The photograph on the left shows destruction in the Piazza Fontana in Milan after an unusually heavy raid.

NEW LANDINGS ON ITALIAN COAST. On 9 September, as the Eighth Army captured Taranto, a new Allied landing was made in the Salerno area, about thirty miles south of Naples. This operation was carried out by the Fifth Army, which included about equal numbers of American and British divisions, and the mighty force sailed from many African ports under the protection of the Allied Navies. Unlike the earlier landings in the extreme south of Italy, troops at Salerno encountered very determined enemy opposition right from the start, the Germans

having had the opportunity to concentrate large forces in the area. During the first day the Fifth Army had to fight off five strong enemy counter-attacks in the course of a violent battle lasting from dawn to dusk. Strong support for our land forces was given by British and American warships offshore. Severe fighting continued throughout next day when Salerno was captured by British troops. The drawing on these pages by Charles Cundall, A.R.A., gives a vivid impression of the landings on Salerno beaches covered by cruisers and destroyers of the Allied Navies.

ITALIAN FLEET SURRENDERS

11 SEPTEMBER, 1943

On the morning of 11 September, Admiral Cunningham announced in an official statement that "the Italian battle fleet is now anchored under the guns of Malta." After the representatives of Marshal Badoglio had signed an armistice with the Allies three days previously, units of the Italian fleet left Taranto, Spezia and various other ports and sailed for Malta, where they arrived on 10 September, flying the Italian colours and the black pennants which were the agreed marks of identification. Four Italian battleships, six cruisers and seven destroyers arrived at Malta that day; four Italian admirals were with their ships. The convoy was heavily bombed by German Stukas and torpedo-bombers in the straits between Corsica and Sardinia in an attempt to prevent the ships reaching Malta, and before it had been provided with Allied air cover, the battleship "Roma" was sunk by a direct hit which split her in two. Survivors were picked up by other Italian warships. Heavy and accurate Italian A.A. fire soon drove the aircraft off and one was destroyed. A huge crowd including Admiral Cunningham and General Eisenhower watched the Italian Fleet enter Valetta. Messages of congratulation were sent to Admiral Cunningham by the King, the Board of Admiralty and General Eisenhower. Admiral Cunningham said: "These ships now added to our strength are first class; and now that the Mediterranean is cleared, it will release many ships for use against the Japanese." Italian submarines kept appearing from various ports and two days after the main Italian fleet had arrived at Malta it was joined by the battleship "Guilo Cesare," which had steamed all the way from Venice to join the Allies. On 12 September, seven battleships arrived in the Balearics, five of which were interned for overstaying the twenty-four hours permitted in a neutral port. More arrived in Bone, Algeria. The picture shows the Italian fleet steaming towards the port of Valetta.

MUSSOLINI RELEASED BY GERMANS. Since the overthrow of the former Italian dictator on 24 July, he had been kept a prisoner in the Gran Sasso Hotel in the Abruzzi Mountains north of Rome. On 12 September Berlin radio announced that German parachutists and armed S.S. men had "carried out an operation for the liberation of Mussolini." The pictures on these pages show: left, Mussolini leaving the hotel surrounded by the German parachutists who freed him from captivity; above, Mussolini saying good-bye to Hitler before returning to Italy.

Fifth Army strengthens

HEAVY FIGHTING AT SALERNO. For several days the struggle at Salerno continued with unabated violence, the Germans launching one counter-attack after another in a frantic attempt to prevent the Fifth Army establishing a bridgehead and to drive them back into the sea. On 12 September the Germans launched particularly heavy counter-attacks with large tank forces supported by fierce artillery fire from well-entrenched positions on high ground overlooking the Allied bridgehead. Despite these and yet fiercer attempts to drive the Fifth Army back, however, strong British and American reinforcements of men and equipment were landed on the Salerno beaches and the bridgehead was maintained. By 16 September the battle was going in favour of the Fifth Army, which had now resumed the offensive, and by the end of that day the Germans had begun a withdrawal. Meanwhile the Eighth Army had been making rapid progress from the south-east towards the southern end of the Salerno front, where, on 17 September, their armoured cars linked up with Fifth Army troops near Ayropoti. The Germans now began their general withdrawal north-west towards Naples Top left, Allied soldiers guarding German prisoners at Salerno; below left, British troops coming ashore at Salerno; above, scene on the beach during landings.

ALLIED PROGRESS AT SALERNO.　On 19 September the Fifth Army gained more ground on the Salerno front, and Battipaglia and Altavilla were captured. Possession was thus gained of the dominating hills of the Sorrento Peninsula.　Great numbers of troops were continually landed under strong naval and air cover.　Enemy tank formations were broken up several times by big naval guns. The Germans were fighting delaying actions. R.A.F. pilots reported that long lines of enemy tanks and lorries were retreating to the north and north-west.　These

were heavily bombed, but the Germans put up little opposition. On 23 September the Fifth Army under Lieutenant-General Clark began a new offensive to the north of Salerno and advanced slowly but steadily against considerable enemy forces. During the following days the Fifth Army's advance was slowed down by the intractable country and heavy demolitions. The photographs show: left, a Vickers machine gun team in the mountainous country north-west of Salerno; above, a 155-mm. howitzer of the United States Army in action in woods near Monte Corvino.

ALLIES ADVANCE TO THE PLAIN OF NAPLES. By 25 September the Fifth Army had reached the Plain of Naples. The advance had been very difficult, since enemy machine gun posts in the mountainous country which it traversed had to be mopped up. On 26 September Calabritto and Caserno were captured and many enemy strong points reduced. Opposition was lighter nearer the coast than farther inland where the enemy had strongly entrenched himself in the Apennines. Meanwhile the Eighth Army had captured Muro, crossed the Ofanto River, and occupied Margherita di Savoia and Cerignola. On the same day it reached the Apulian Plain twenty miles from the great Foggia air base which the enemy had recently evacuated. On 27-28 September the Fifth Army again advanced and fought some of the fiercest actions of the Italian campaign amid appalling weather conditions. A German line from Castellammare to Nocera was smashed and Camerelle was captured. Support was given by guns of the Royal Navy offshore. The sudden collapse of the enemy was very extraordinary, as he had hitherto fought most stubbornly. The morale of enemy prisoners captured was poor. The pictures show: above, fighting at close quarters on the Plain of Naples. British soldiers are seen passing a wrecked German tank; left, an American soldier reading abandoned German newspapers in a deserted and broken enemy tent.

FIFTH ARMY ENTERS NAPLES

On 29 September the enemy ring which held up the advance of the Fifth Army was destroyed and Vesuvius was the only height remaining in the hands of the Germans between Nocera and Naples. Field Marshal Kesselring ordered a retreat covered by extensive demolitions. In Naples all port installations, warehouses and everything that would be of use to the Allied troops, was wrecked, besides many non-military buildings. With the improvement of the weather, the Allied air forces resumed the heavy bombing of enemy troops, transports and road bridges. Five divisions were safely withdrawn from Naples by the enemy, but a rearguard, including some of Germany's best troops, was wiped out. At 8 a.m. on 1 October advanced troops of the Fifth Army entered Naples. They received a most enthusiastic welcome from the people. After the widespread destruction in Naples by the Germans, a serious typhus epidemic broke out and General Clark, Commander of the Fifth Army, was forced to put the whole city out of bounds except for those on essential war service. Sappers who had worked on the demolished harbours in Tripoli, Tunisia and Sicily subsequently made the harbour at Naples usable again although the Germans had stated that all installations of military importance had been thoroughly destroyed. The photograph on these pages shows the Neapolitans greeting the Allied forces.

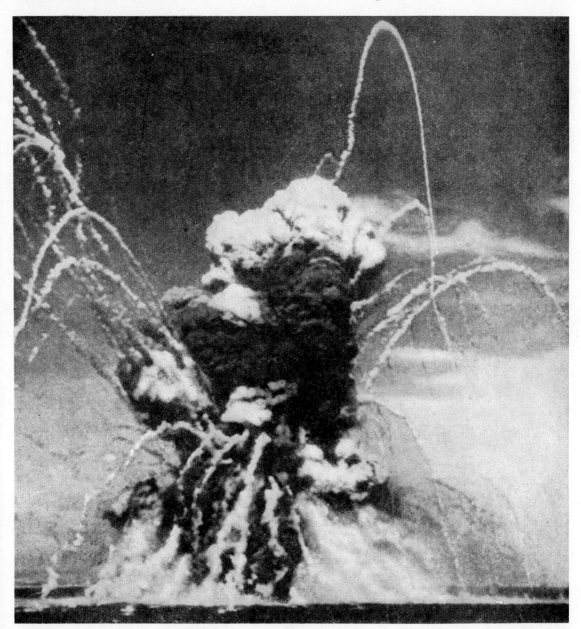

ATTACKS BY BRITISH LIGHT CRAFT. On 10 October Mr. Churchill and President Roosevelt stated that "until the third week in September no Allied ship was lost by German U-boat attack." The lull had been broken, however, on 19 September when a pack of about fifteen U-boats attacked a west-bound convoy. There was a running fight lasting four and a half days and three escort vessels were sunk besides a few merchant ships. A large number of submarines were sunk, however, as a result of vigorous surface and air counter-attacks. Increased fighter protection was being used by our convoys and motor gun boats were helping to make their passage even safer. These ships are both fast (being able to attain a speed of 50 m.p.h.) and very heavily armed for their size. These "little ships" scored a notable victory on 24 October when thirty E boats made an attempt to waylay a convoy in the North Sea. They were engaged by M.G.B.s in a running fight which lasted nearly five hours. None of our ships was lost, while four of the enemy were sunk and six damaged. Top left, return to harbour of M.G.B.s with German prisoners. Bottom left, some survivors of the crew of a merchant ship torpedoed by an enemy submarine. The photograph was taken from a United States naval blimp, which dropped a rubber life dinghy seen in the picture. Above, result of a direct hit by a German dive bomber on an American cargo-carrying ship.

SUCCESSES IN NEW GUINEA. By early October the Japanese were in full retreat up the Ramu Valley in the north of New Guinea. Allied control of the air bases in this area constituted a further threat to Japanese sea communications with the important base of Rabaul, which was being continually harassed by the Allies from the air. Left, troops supervised by military engineers harnessing a river along which a new road is being built; above, a bridge is being built in the South Pacific while a machine gunner keeps watch for Japanese patrols and snipers.

41

AIR WAR IN THE PACIFIC. While the Japanese were being dislodged from the Solomons and New Guinea, their air bases and sea communications were being relentlessly bombed. In early October Allied air forces had been making a series of successful raids over places on the Bandu, the Flores and the Timor Seas. Japanese communications which had to connect up over an enormous area were made increasingly difficult to operate. Left, native porters in New Guinea carry supplies. Above, a bomb from an Allied plane hits a barge containing oil.

FIFTH ARMY ADVANCES FROM NAPLES. By the evening of 1 October British armoured formations of the Fifth Army were already advancing some miles north of Naples, pursuing the Germans back to new defence lines on the Volturno River. Allied air forces bombed the retreating enemy columns incessantly. The two biggest aerodromes in Italy, Capodichino and Pomigliano, fell into Allied hands with the capture of Naples. The photographs show: above, the Allies entering Naples; right, an Italian policeman gives an American soldier a drink.

CORSICA SET FREE

Before the Italian Armistice was signed about 15,000 Corsican patriots were secretly armed by the Allies. On 8 September, when news of the Italian surrender was received, there was a general rising. Vichy officials were arrested in almost all towns and villages. There were clashes with German troops in the mountains near Sartene and the enemy was forced to withdraw to Bastia and Bonifacio. General Giraud broadcast a message to the German High Command in Corsica declaring that anyone wearing a white brassard on his arm embroidered with a Moor's head (part of the arms of Corsica) must be considered as a regular soldier of the French Army and not treated as an armed civilian if captured. By 21 September the western half of Corsica was in French hands. German bases on the island, including the important airfield at Bastia, were heavily bombed by the Allied air forces. The food shortage, already very serious, was further intensified when the Germans set fire to about 1,000 acres of crops and farmsteads. By 5 October the enemy was finally cleared from Corsica. The recapture of Corsica was important not only because it might be used by the enemy as a U-boat base but it gave the Allies an important base for air and amphibious operations. This photograph shows remains of German war material at Bastia in Corsica after the enemy had left the island.

PASSAGE OF THE VOLTURNO. On 2 October the Fifth Army advanced north of Naples towards the Volturno River, hampered by enemy rearguard actions, demolitions, mines and swollen mountain torrents. Despite the difficulties very rapid progress was made, and on 8 October the Volturno was crossed by advanced infantry and artillery units. On 13 October an offensive was launched after an intense barrage from over 500 guns. Troops crossed the river in every type of boat and craft, and by swimming, under a fierce hail of enemy mortar and machine gun fire. The photographs show: top right, Allied gun position in the garden of King Victor Emmanuel's palace at Caserta; bottom right, Allied 3.7 A.A. guns in action at night; above, the crossing of the Volturno.

AIR ATTACKS ON GERMAN INDUSTRIES

On 8-10 October the British and American Air Forces carried out extensive raids on Germany. On 8 October, Fortresses attacked by day the shipyards and aircraft factories at Bremen and the U-boat slips at Vegesack causing much damage. Heavy opposition was met over the target area and at least 140 German fighters were shot down for the loss of thirty Fortresses and three of their fighter escort. The same night, the R.A.F. attacked Bremen and Hanover in great strength and many fires were left burning in the industrial quarters of both cities. On the following day American planes kept up the offensive with attacks against the Focke-Wulf assembly plant at Marienburg. Shipbuilding yards, oil-storage tanks and other objectives at Danzig were also destroyed. On 10 October, the U.S.A.A.F. bombed Munster. Great fires were left burning and 102 German fighters were destroyed for the loss of thirty bombers and two fighters. The same day, the Air Ministry announced that in the course of extensive damage caused by the raids of 9 August, 5 September, 23 September, 100 industrial plants of great importance to Germany were destroyed. Amongst these was the Heinrich Lanz plant, turning out tank parts and army tractors, which was entirely destroyed. In addition the main stations at Mannheim and Ludwigshafen were hit. The photograph shows a street in an industrial city of Germany devastated by heavy Allied raids.

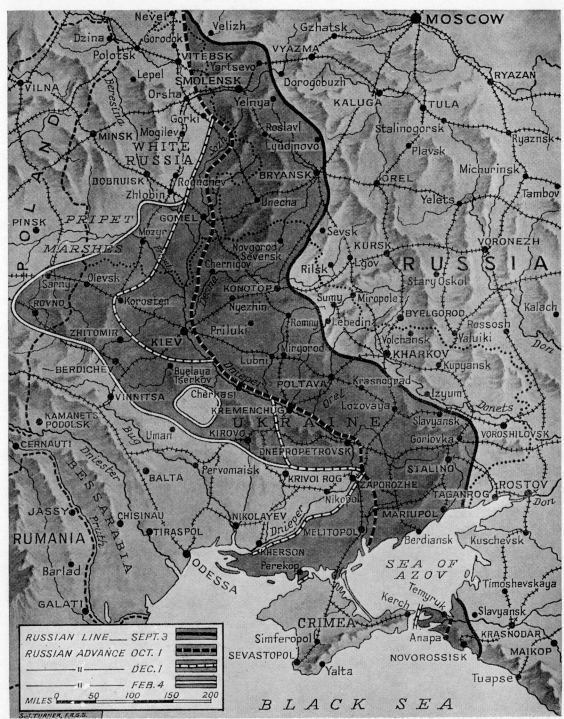

RUSSIAN ADVANCES. On 7 October the Russians, after pausing for a week to bring up reserves, announced the resumption of an offensive on a 1,000 mile front from Vitebsk to the Taman Peninsula. On the same day, two other gains were made in addition to the capture of the great centre of Nevel. These consisted of the forcing of the middle Dnieper in three places and the wiping out of the German bridgeheads in the Taman Peninsula. The map, drawn by S. J. Turner, F.R.G.S., shows the Russian advances between 3 September and 4 February.

CAPTURE OF NEVEL AND LIOZNO. On 7 October the Red Army captured the important railway junction of Nevel and the town of Liozno, an important stronghold east of Vitebsk. In the Gomel region, Dobruzh, twelve miles east of Gomel, was retaken. Berlin spokesmen considered the reverses in these areas very serious, since German reserves were being used up very rapidly and their northern armies in danger of being cut off or having to retreat very quickly across difficult ground. Above, Russian refugees hurry past the body of a dead German.

RED ARMY BEFORE GOMEL AND KIEV. On 11 October the Red Army was again advancing, and in the Kiev region two divisions succeeded in breaking through and recapturing many localities. Kiev was now seriously threatened and the Germans suffered huge casualties in an attempt to hold the city. Moscow radio announced that the German line north of the city had been smashed. By 13 October, although the weather had broken and turned the roads into quagmires, Russian troops broke through the German lines and were fighting before Gomel itself.

The Red Air Force had gained complete air superiority and the Germans, after their losses in machines, were driven to using old and obsolete types of aircraft. Meanwhile, the Germans were suffering very heavy casualties in an attempt to hold Kiev at all costs. Battles were raging all over the city and the Red Air Force had complete air superiority. Refugees had terrible stories to tell of wanton destruction and cruelty by Germans in both Gomel and Kiev. The photograph shows Russian peasants encamped for the night on their way to slavery in Germany.

ZAPOROZHE RECAPTURED BY RED ARMY. On 14 October the Russians won back the city of Zaporozhe. The enemy admitted that they had been forced to evacuate the city and they suffered hundreds of casualties, most of whom were drowned trying to cross to the right bank of the Dnieper. Above, the Germans retreat down muddy roads; top right, a German soldier looks at the ruin of a bridge over the Dnieper destroyed after the last German column had crossed; bottom right, the Germans in retreat, burning everything before them as they go.

KIEV
RECAPTURED

By 29 October General Tolbukhin had advanced on a forty-five mile front leaving Melitopol seventy miles in the rear. Owing to the speed of the advance, the Germans were being thrown into disorganized groups and an enormous amount of booty was taken. On 31 October the Russians were only fifteen miles from the Perekop isthmus and the German forces in the Crimea were threatened with complete isolation. Russian units were pouring into the Crimea and on 1 November the enemy's last land retreat from the Crimea was cut off by the capture of Perekop and Armiansk on the road and railway leading to Simferopol and Sevastopol. Between 31 October and 1 November 6,000 prisoners were taken. On the lower Dnieper, the Germans were in full retreat pursued by Cossacks and it appeared that they were in grave danger of losing Kherson. On 2 November Kakhova, forty miles above Kherson, was captured and some thousands of Germans were killed attempting to cross the river. On 6 November Kiev, the third largest city in Russia and a great industrial centre, was captured, after being in German hands for over two years. Left, a German supply column. Below, Nazi troops widen a road to hasten communications.

Americans launch attac

U.S. MARINES LAND ON TARAWA. On 20 November American Marines under Rear-Admiral Harry W. Hill and Major-General Julian C. Smith landed on the important Japanese air base of Tarawa in the Gilbert Islands. In spite of terrific enemy fire, they almost exterminated the garrison, which fought with fanatical courage. The American casualties in the assaults on the Gilbert Islands were heavy and the battles were among the bloodiest in the present war. In the seventy-six hours' fighting the Americans suffered 1,025 killed and 2,257 wounded,

while the enemy lost about 5,000. Five hundred strongly defended pillboxes had to be stormed and taken, and these had been so arranged that each one when taken was open to cross-fire from two others. They were very strongly constructed of coco-nut logs between two thick walls of sand, concrete and steel. In addition, there was heavy fire from machine guns, each of which commanded a whole beach, and from tree-top snipers. The picture shows U.S. marines taking such shelter as they can find behind shattered palm trees on the beach of Tarawa.

OCCUPATION OF THE GILBERTS BY U.S. FORCES. On 22 November United States troops had improved their positions in Tarawa, where mopping-up operations were continuing to destroy a few isolated enemy strong points. The fighting had been so severe that of the 3,000 U.S. Marines who had made the first assault, only a few hundred remained alive, although U.S. battleships, cruisers and destroyers shelled the island with 2,000 tons of shells while aircraft dropped 800 bombs on enemy positions. Owing to a coral reef impeding the landing barges, the Marines were forced to wade the last 800 yards to the shore under a murderous fire from heavy machine guns, rifles and mortars. After having landed, they had to scale five-foot barricades of coco-nut-palm logs. Behind the barricades were pillboxes of concrete and steel. An attack was also made in the rear by Iapanese soldiers hidden in wrecked hulks. The following day Betio, the key to Tarawa atoll, was taken after a

decisive action in which 4,000 Japanese were annihilated in fierce and unsuccessful counter-attacks. Makin and Abemama, other Gilbert islands, were taken much more easily. Colonel Knox in Washington said that the attacks on the Gilbert Islands had two objectives: (1) to drive the Japanese from mandated territories; (2) to shorten U.S. supply routes in the South-West Pacific by hundreds of miles. The landings were the beginning of a campaign to open a more direct route (across the South-West Pacific) to Japan, and, for a beginning, the Marshall Islands were thereby seriously threatened. No Japanese surface vessels were seen during the operations; but after the battles, U.S. carrier-borne aircraft operating in the Gilberts shot down thirty-four Japanese fighters, nine bombers and four seaplanes for the loss of three fighters and one bomber. Only a very small number of Japanese prisoners were taken. The picture shows the shattered beach of Tarawa after the end of the fierce battle.

FIGHTING ON THE PRIPET MARSHES

On 27 November there was heavy fighting on a 100-mile front near the Pripet Marshes. The Germans, trying to retreat towards Poland, were much hampered by the nature of the country. They were forced to build wooden tracks over which light loads could be pulled in horse-drawn vehicles. Top left, a flooded highway over the Pripet Marshes with wrecked vehicles lining roadside. Bottom left, German soldiers cut off by Red Army await relief. Top right, German transport column of horse-drawn wagons crosses Pripet Marshes over a wooden track. Bottom right, retreating Germans leave a town in flames.

RECAPTURE OF CHANGTEH

On 25 November, the Japanese, making considerable use of paratroops, had captured and taken possession of the city of Changteh, important as the centre of the rice-producing district. On 27 November, a very heavy counter-attack was launched and over 5,000 of the enemy were killed. The Chinese had succeeded in cutting off all communications excepting one over Lake Tungting and another by trail skirting the lake's western shores. It was alleged that the enemy were making use of poison-gas shells. On 30 November, bitter hand-to-hand fighting was taking place in the streets of the city. By 1 December, the Chinese forces under General Yu Cheng-Wan supported by American aircraft drove the enemy entirely from the city. The Japanese retreated to a point two miles north. By 3 December, the city had again fallen into the hands of the Japanese. Less than 300 men of the Chinese 57th Division survived. On 9 December, the city changed hands yet again, and General Hseuh Yeuk stated that the Chinese had suffered very heavily in the action, their losses far exceeding those of the enemy. But the importance of the city was such that it was felt it must be retaken at all costs. The picture (by permission of "The Times" shows Chinese refugees re-entering Changteh.

JUNGLE FIGHTING IN NEW GUINEA

In New Guinea, on 1 December, the Australians were advancing in three directions on Wareo, an important trail junction eleven miles to the north-east of Settelberg. A suspension bridge over the Song River was seized and next day, Kuanko, only half a mile away from Wareo, was captured after fierce jungle fighting. On 5 December, the Japanese launched a series of determined counter-attacks but these were routed by accurate artillery fire. Three days later the Australians took Wareo and pursued the enemy some distance north. The advance on Madang, some forty miles up the coast, now commenced. Weather conditions were appalling and torrential rain drove the Japanese from a number of strong defensive positions. A mile and a half north of Wareo two more Australian columns were able to link up on the Bonga-Wareo trail. From this point, the advance became very slow owing to the difficult nature of the country and heavy rain storms, but on 15 December the village of Lukona was captured. The picture shows natives of New Guinea acting as stretcher bearers and carrying an Australian soldier through the dense jungle. Only a short time ago these natives were completely savage, being head-hunters and cannibals, but the present war has done much to bring at least a veneer of civilization to them.

ON THE OUTSKIRTS OF ZHLOBIN. On 2 December Russian patrols were on the outskirts of Zhlobin, which was being very fiercely defended by the enemy. The weather conditions continued bad with snow and sleet, but the Red Army launched a determined offensive to clear the enemy out of White Russia. Strong German reinforcements were hurried to the scene in a vain effort to stem General Rokossovsky's advance. On 4 December the first German war criminal was condemned by court martial and hanged on the same tree where he himself had ordered many executions. Top left, a Russian tank, carrying troops, breaks through German position; bottom left, soldiers of the Red Army press through a liberated Russian town on their way westwards; above, a German supply column moves forward with difficulty; below, Red Army mobile guns go into action. Infantry are descending from an armoured vehicle in the background while guns of another tank engage the enemy.

MEETINGS OF
ALLIED STATESMEN

On 21 November, President Roosevelt, Generalissimo Chiang Kai-Shek and Mr. Churchill met in North Africa for the purpose of issuing a statement on Allied policy regarding the war against Japan. After leaving Nor.h Africa, Mr. Churchill and President Roosevelt travelled to Teheran, the capital of Iran, to meet Marshal Stalin. This conference lasted from 28 November to 1 December. A joint statement declared that the Allies had come to full agreement concerning the timing of all military operations. Top left, Generalissimo Chiang Kai-Shek, President Roosevelt, Mr. Churchill and Mme Chiang Kai-Shek in North Africa. Bottom left, Marshal Stalin, President Roosevelt and Mr. Churchill at Teheran. Behind are M. Molotov, Mrs. Oliver (Mr. Churchill's daughter) and Mr. Anthony Eden. Top right, the presentation of the Stalingrad sword. Marshal Voroshilov shows the sword to President Roosevelt. Bottom right, ceremony of presentation.

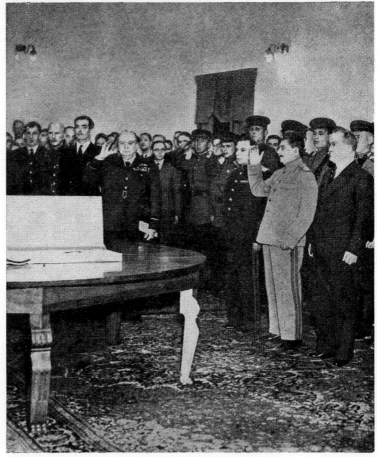

FIERCE FIGHTING IN WHITE RUSSIA

On 3-4 December, although the weather still continued bad with heavy slee and rain, there was very severe fighting in White Russia. In the Gomel area many localities were captured by the Red Army in spite of strong enemy resistance, including Dovsk, an important junction of roads eading to Rogachev, Mogilev and Propoisk, the river port of Sverzhen and Staraya Rudnya. Zhlobin and Rogachev were seriously threatened. On the following day a very rap:d advance was carr'ed out a ong a 250-mile front stretching from the Vitebsk-Orsha area in the north to the Rogachev area in the south. In spite of a heavy snow storm, determined and desperate counter-attacks were beaten off and a number of strong points were captured 'ncluding Khalch, only eight miles from Zhlobin and on the Gomel-Zhlobin railway. The following day the fall of snow was so heavy that only mobile units were able to operate but, in spite of this, substantial gains were made and several localities were retaken. Local partisans played a very important part in these operations. The picture shows Nazi troops retreating through a Russian town in an attempt to disengage from forward units of the Red Army.

GERMAN THRUST TOWARDS KIEV. On 6 December the Germans admitted that they had carried out a "disengaging" movement in the Dnieper bend in face of superior Russian forces. General Koniev's forces advanced rapidly, cut the Znamenka-Symela line, and took eighteen enemy fortified positions. The next day Field Marshal von Manstein massed between 1,200 and 1,700 tanks in an attempt to destroy the Russians in the Kiev salient. A fierce battle started near Chernyakhov, where the Germans overcame several villages and strong positions. The following day they advanced twenty-five miles toward Kiev and the Sixth Rumanian Cavalry division under Lieutenant-General Teodorini broke the Soviet bridgehead to the south of Kerch. Two thousand prisoners were taken, and light German naval forces destroyed seven Russian ships evacuating Russian soldiers from Kerch. Left, a German tank column on the move; above, German prisoners marched into captivity.

ZNAMENKA CAPTURED BY THE RED ARMY. On 9 December General Koniev's troops advanced inside the Dnieper bend and captured several German strong-points including the village of Novaya Praga, where a fierce battle was fought and 2,000 Germans killed. By the capture of Mederovo, the important railway junction of Znamenka was surrounded. The powerful triple rings of enemy defences were destroyed by concentrated artillery fire and, on the following day, tanks and infantry poured in, annihilated the garrison, and captured the

city. On the same day General Koniev's forces pushed rapidly on in the direction of Kirovograd, the important industrial town to the south-west of Znamenka. Later in the day spearheads of the Red Army were within twenty miles of Kirovograd. Late frost greatly added to their mobility, and the German High Command was forced to admit that their front had been materially shortened in the Znamenka area owing to pressure by far superior forces. The picture shows Russian peasants returning to their homes, from which they had been driven by the invader.

RABAUL ATTACKED. For some time Rabaul, the capital of New Britain and an important naval and air base in the hands of the enemy, was subjected to intensive Allied bombing and to bombardment from the sea. The enemy were striving desperately to hold it at all costs. Between October and the beginning of January Allied aircraft bombed Rabaul seventeen times and, swooping over Simpson harbour, destroyed Japanese shipping, warehouses and harbour installations. The airfields at Vuno, Kanan, Rapopo and Tobera nearby were badly hit. In the course of these attacks, the Japanese lost about 140 ships and 700 planes. Above, a Japanese transport sinking after having received a hit from an Allied bomber. Top right, a United States carrier defends herself against Japanese aircraft. Bottom right, an enemy plane falls flaming into the sea after being hit by the carrier's A.A. fire.

BITTER FIGHTING ON THE MORO

By 10 December, the Allies had already crossed the Moro at Frisa, seven miles from Ortona, and had established a bridgehead on the far bank. That same day the village o San Leonardo was taken and there was fierce fighting in the outskirts of Ortona and Orsogna. Enemy counter-attacks were unsuccessful owing to bad weather. On 12 December, the Allies had advanced to the hills overlooking Ortona and to within two miles of the city. Weather conditions continued appalling, with rain and mud. The Germans, who were dug in on a fifteen-mile front, launched heavy and repeated counter-attacks, all of which were repulsed. A terrific artillery duel followed; and, a little distance inland, a slight advance was made by the Indians, who took some prisoners. On 14 December, the bridgehead on the Moro had been enlarged to a strip five miles long. In unsuccessful counter-attacks, 200 German prisoners were taken. Canadian patrols entered the German-occupied village of Berardi and captured the commanding officer, four other officers and 140 men of a Panzer Grenadier Regiment, together with a quantity of equipment. On the next day the village of Berardi was taken and the Ortona-Orsogna Road was cut in several places. The picture shows troops of the Eighth Army making their way over a snow covered hillside.

ORTONA TAKEN BY THE EIGHTH ARMY. By 17 December, the Allies were seriously threatening Orsogna and Ortona; the Germans, in an attempt to hold them at all costs, threw tanks and paratroops into the defence. Thirteen enemy tanks were destroyed, two more were captured and many prisoners were taken. In the early hours of next morning, the Canadians attacked after a heavy artillery bombardment in which 70,000 shells were poured into the German positions. Allied tanks afterwards broke through the German lines, meeting little opposition

and taking the village of Poggiofiorito. In the attempt to hold Ortona and Orsogna the German 90th Panzer Grenadier Division was wiped out. On 19 December, British troops supported by tanks made a short advance but were
held up by machine gunners entrenched in the olive groves. During the course of the next few days, the Germans
held every cottage and house in the route of the Eighth Army with great determination; but on 23 December, the
Canadians were in Ortona. Picture shows one of the rain-sodden artillery posts from which Ortona was shelled.

DESTRUCTION OF THE "SCHARNHORST." On 26 December the German battleship "Scharnhorst" attempted to attack a Russia-bound convoy but was engaged by units of the Home Fleet. The "Scharnhorst" was seen in the twilight of an Arctic morning south-east of Bear Island sailing in the direction of the convoy. She was attacked by H.M.S. "Norfolk" and steamed off at full speed. A few hours later she again attempted to intercept the convoy but was driven off to the Norwegian coast. All that afternoon she was followed by cruisers and destroyers and her position reported to H.M.S. "Duke of York." Towards afternoon the "Duke of York" contacted the enemy and scored a direct hit below her waterline which greatly reduced her speed. In spite of this, she evaded the "Duke

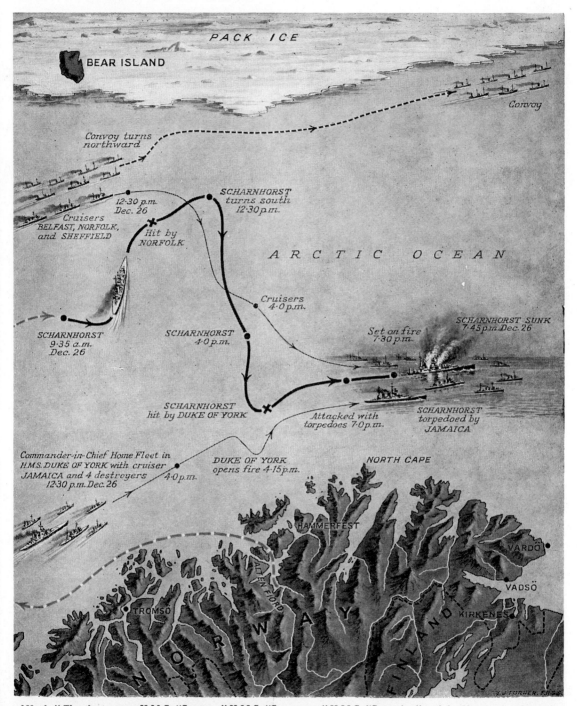

PACK ICE

BEAR ISLAND

Convoy

Convoy turns
northward

SCHARNHORST
turns south
12·30 p.m.

12·30 p.m.
Dec. 26

Cruisers
BELFAST, NORFOLK,
and SHEFFIELD

Hit by
NORFOLK

A R C T I C   O C E A N

Cruisers
4·0 p.m.

SCHARNHORST SUNK
7·45 p.m. Dec. 26

Set on fire
7·30 p.m.

SCHARNHORST
9·35 a.m.
Dec. 26

SCHARNHORST
4·0 p.m.

SCHARNHORST
hit by DUKE OF YORK

Attacked with
torpedoes 7·0 p.m.

SCHARNHORST
torpedoed by
JAMAICA

Commander-in-Chief Home Fleet in
H.M.S. DUKE OF YORK with cruiser
JAMAICA and 4 destroyers
12·30 p.m. Dec. 26

4·0 p.m.

DUKE OF YORK
opens fire 4·15 p.m.

NORTH CAPE

HAMMERFEST

VARDÖ

VADSÖ

TROMSÖ

ALTEN FIORD

N O R W A Y

KIRKENES

F I N L A N D

S. J. TURNER, F.R.G.S.

of York." The destroyers H.M.S. "Savage," H.M.S. "Saumarez," H.M.S. "Scorpion" and the Norwegian destroyer
"Stord" followed her and, unsupported, attacked her with torpedoes. Shortly afterwards, four other destroyers
closed in and scored torpedo hits which so reduced the speed of the "Scharnhorst" that the "Duke of York"
was able to close in. The "Scharnhorst" attempted to escape by altering her course, but was unable to evade
the "Duke of York" which hammered her with her 14-in. guns and turned her into a burning wreck. The final
blow was struck by H.M.S. "Jamaica" which sank the "Scharnhorst" by torpedo. The convoy proceeded unharmed.
Left shows the "Scharnhorst" and above, the map, drawn by S. J. Turner, shows the course of the running fight.

GERMANS DESTROY AN ITALIAN TOWN

28 DECEMBER, 1943

Throughout the next few days bitter fighting continued in Ortona. On 27 December, the Canadians were mopping up the centres of resistance and clearing blockhouses. Furious but unsuccessful counter-attacks were launched, in which the Germans used flame throwers. On the following day, the Canadians were in full occupation of the now ruined town after nine days' hard fighting. Casualties, both military and civilian were very heavy during the fighting and the Germans, before they left, filled the town with booby traps. At the end of the day, the Canadians were pursuing the enemy up the Adriatic Coast in the direction of Pescara. On 29 December, the Canadians advanced north of Ortona over roads which had been extensively mined and demolished by the enemy. Meanwhile enemy artillery shelled Ortona from the hills. Local gains were made by Indian troops between Ortona and Orsogna. By 31 December the Eighth Army had advanced to a point within eight miles of Pescara in the face of mines, demolitions and heavy fire from mortars and machine guns. The advance was further impeded by heavy rain and high winds and the Germans fought hard to defend every yard. On 2 January the weather was so bad with snow blizzards, rain and high wind that activity was limited to patrolling. There was, however, some stubborn fighting on the coast road leading to Pescara where the Canadians were attacking German troops holding a high ridge. These were finally dislodged. Next day, the weather improved and the Canadians were able to make further advances, meeting with stubborn resistance between Ortona and Pescara. Indian troops captured some high ground a few miles west of Ortona and were in command of the coastal road to Chieti at a point two miles from Tollo. The picture shows the ruins of an Italian town blown up by retreating Germans. Italian peasants can be seen trying to salvage all that remains of their possessions and homes.

ADVANCE ON CASSINO

On 7 January, after violent hand-to-hand fighting, the village of San Vittore was occupied by the Americans. A swift advance now started and by 11 January the Allies were before Monte Trocchio, the last important height before Cassino. The following day Cervaro, the enemy stronghold guarding the way to Cassino, was captured. On 14 January the outer defences of Monte Trocchio were attacked and the Gustav line defending Cassino heavily bombarded. Top, Allied engineers rebuilding a damaged bridge over a river. Left, 25-pounder guns in action. Right, amphibious "ducks" cross the Sangro River.

MOUNTAIN AND RIVER FIGHTING. On 21 January the Americans crossed the Rapido in boats and established a bridgehead on the north bank of the river near San Angelo, three miles from Cassino. The next day Allied troops landed at Anzio, the port for Nettuno, behind the enemy's lines and fifty miles above the Fifth Army's front line on the Garigliano. Nettuno was taken before the Germans had time to demolish it and the Allies pushed on eight miles up the Appian Way, the road to Rome. Above, German prisoners. Right, Allied troops advance in mountains.

GUSTAV LINE
REACHED

Throughout the day and night of 24 anuary men and war ma erial were poured into the small port of Anzio on the Nettuno br dgehead. The Germans launched fierce attacks against the Allies but these were repulsed and advances made. American roops reached the Gustav Line south of Cassino, where they clashed with enemy patro s. The next day they crossed the Rapido River under a smoke screen and advanced in the area north of Cassino over enemy minefields and on to the outposts of the Gustav Line. French roops, under General Juin, were advancing over difficult ground and under intense fire only five miles from Cassino. They crossed the Secco River (a tributary of the Garigliano) and attempted to capture the Belvedere ridge, to which a captured order of the day from Hitler attached very great importance. On 28 January a considerable area of important ground was captured and some determined enemy counterattacks were repulsed. The next day the French captured three important heights. Meanwhile, the progress of the Americans in the Gustav Line had been somewhat slowed by the fact that the enemy had dynamited the banks of the Rapido, thus, not only diverting its course, but flooding the area along which supplies could be brought. On the Garigliano the British made rapid progress and captured important high ground on Monte Turlito. During these operations the Allied air forces relentlessly bombed the town of Cassino, which stood in the way of the Allied advance on Rome. The picture shows the devastating effect o these bombings.

DEEPENING THE ANZIO BEACHHEAD

The Germans had been caught quite unprepared for the landings at Anzio on 22 January and there was almost no enemy resistance although extensive demolition preparations had been made. These, however, were not put into operation. Indeed so hurried had been the enemy's retreat that the villas and hotels of Nettuno were left quite undamaged. Meanwhile fresh troops and stores were poured into the Anzio beachhead which had reached a depth of six miles inland by 24 January. The Germans rushed reinforcements to the area in an effort to prevent the further landings which were taking place under powerful naval and air cover. By 26 January the beachhead was about the size of the Isle of Wight. A factory, converted by the enemy into a strong-point, was stormed and a hundred prisoners taken. During the course of the next few days very considerable advance was made under a powerful barrage. On 29 January the town of Carroceto was captured. Pictures show, top, infantry coming ashore at Anzio under smoke screen; bottom, bren-gun carriers being landed.

ATTACK ON GUSTAV LINE. On 30 January the 5th Army made a considerable advance along the lower reaches of the Garigliano and captured two important heights. Meanwhile, the Americans crossed the Rapido with tanks and after three days' fighting breached the defences of the Gustav Line. With the support of heavy artillery extensive enemy entanglements and strong-points were destroyed. Next day further breaches were made in the Gustav Line and the village of Cairo was captured. The pictures show, left, a British soldier kicking in a door which a companion keeps covered. Above, the town of Cassino shelled by American artillery.

ATTACK ON
MARSHALL ISLANDS

On 1 February an American force, under the command of Vice-Admiral Spruance, launched an attack on the Marshall Islands. After a concentrated bombardment by U.S. warships and aerial bombing by carrier and shore-based aircraft, U.S. infantry and marines landed in the Kwajalein and Roi areas. Allied air attacks were also made on Maloelap, Mili and Jaluit. These operations were the biggest yet carried out in the Pacific. Next day, there were landings on Namur Island, and on 4 February Admiral Nimitz issued a proclamation to the inhabitants of the Marshalls announcing "the suspension of the powers of the Emperor of Japan" in the islands. Top left, a Japanese aircraft shot down into the sea. Bottom left, U.S. aircraft destroy Japanese supply ship. Below the destruction of a Japanese armed cargo vessel.

REDUCING ENEMY MAN-POWER

On 1 February French and American troops had broken through the Gustav Line on a front several miles long. A German barracks was captured in the village of Monte Villa and many pillboxes and deep dug-outs were destroyed. There was very fierce fighting near the village of Terelle where the French took several heights overlooking Cassino. Next day the Allies were in the outskirts of the town but very stiff resistance was met as the enemy had converted every house into a strong-point. Very bitter house-to-house fighting took place in the now ruined town. The enemy launched many heavy counter-attacks in the mountains north and west of Cassino but these were only partially successful. They regained two small heights on Monte Manna but lost Monte Abate and Monte Albaneta. On 6 February the Americans captured three more heights but one was later retaken by the enemy. In the meantime the Germans were receiving very strong air support and although many formations were successfully broken up, the American positions were very heavily attacked. On 8-9-10 February Allied Air Forces made over 2,000 sorties, which included attacks on Cisterna, Tarquinia, Orveto and Viterbo airfields. "Fortresses" attacked rail yards and other targets at Verona and Siena, shipping at Piombino and enemy troops and transports near Rome. Picture shows German prisoners being marched out of a landing craft on their way to a prison camp.

BOMBING OFFENSIVES INCREASE. At the beginning of February the Luftwaffe resumed bombing raids on Britain. The attacks, on a comparatively weak scale, were directed chiefly against the London area. They were undoubtedly a form of retaliation for the mass attacks launched against the Reich by the powerful British and American air forces. Left, air raid wardens aid rescue work at a bombed nursing home: above, Field Marshal Goering, instigator of the renewed attacks on Britain, visiting bombed areas in the Reich itself.

DESTROYING THE ENEMY ON NAMUR. On 3 February the process of annihilating the enemy was proceeding on Namur Island. The remnants of the Japanese garrison had been trapped. About thirty-six hours after the fall of Namur, a blockhouse on the island was found still to be in the hands of the enemy. Moreover, it was soon discovered that it still contained a somewhat larger garrison than was at first suspected. It was supposed that the occu-

pants had been waiting for a counter-attack when it is presumed they would have emerged and taken part in the renewed fighting. Their strong-point was, however, blown up. The picture shows the capture of those of its occupants who remained alive after the destruction of the blockhouse. One is seen surrendering to the United States Marines, another is seen fighting his way out of the debris, while the body of a third is lying at the foot of the stairs.

OCCUPATION OF THE MARSHALLS. By 5 February the occupation of Kwajalein and Roi was almost complete. The same day the Atoll of Ebeye, important because it contained a seaplane base and a radio station, was in Allied hands. Speaking before the Japanese Imperial Diet, General Tojo said: "The war situation is increasing in gravity day by day. For the first time, the enemy has really attacked Japanese soil." Top left, U.S. infantry on Kwajalein advance. Bottom left, Japanese hide-out destroyed by flame-thrower. Above U.S. Marines wade ashore.

ALLIES BOMB WESTERN EUROPE

During February the Allied Air Forces attacked occupied Europe on a very large scale both by day and night. Improved long-range American twin-fuselaged fighters which accompanied the bombers made it possible to penetrate more deeply into enemy territory. These fighters carried extra petrol tankage, had thirty per cent increase in horse-power, better rate of climb with considerable increase above 30,000 feet and a ceiling of over 40,000 feet. When used as fighter bombers these "Lightnings" carry a heavier bomb load than any other U.S.A.A.F. machine of a similar type. On 5-6 February some of the most important Luftwaffe bases in occupied Europe were severely raided. A force of American heavy bombers escorted by "Thunderbolts," "Lightnings" and "Mustangs" and R.A.F. "Spitfires" attacked targets in the Pas-de-Calais area and enemy repair and operational centres at Evreux-Fauville, Saint-Andre de L'Eure, Caen, Chateaudun and St. Aubin. Very little opposition was met with. Reconnaissance photographs showed that very heavy damage had been done and at least thirty-seven machines destroyed. In addition airfields were attacked at Villaconblay, Orleans-Bricy, Chateauroux, La Mastiniere, Avord and Tours. "Mosquitoes" of the Bomber Command were over Berlin. Mines were also laid in enemy waters. On 8 February, there were further heavy raids. Formations of U.S. "Fortresses" escorted by long-range fighters made a concentrated attack on Frankfurt doing very considerable damage and destroying nineteen fighters. U.S. "Marauders" and "Liberators" and British, Dominion and Allied machines flew about 350 sorties with no losses. During the night R.A.F. "Lancasters" attacked the Gnome-Rhone aero-engine works at Limoges. The attack was carried out in bright moonlight and under a clear sky. Great fires were started and the target was almost obliterated by heavy smoke when the last of the force turned home. A further successful attack on Brunswick, important as the centre of Germany's aircraft industry, was carried out on 10 February by American heavy bombers. Picture shows "Fortresses" flying through flak over Berlin.

END OF JAPANESE FIGHT ON KWAJALEIN

On 6 February mopping up operations were continuing on Kwajalen. The remains of the Japanese garrison was holding out at the north-east of the island on a small stretch 400 yards long. The atolls of Gugegive, Bigej and Elber were captured without opposition on the same day. On 8 February all enemy resistance was at an end. The present victory gave the United States more than eighty islands in the sixty-mile long atoll, "the most important base in the Marshalls," in the words of the Official Washington Statement. Top, American troops are seen landing tanks, trucks, oil drums, ammunition and supplies on Kwajalein. Bottom left, a great geyser of smoke arises from a Japanese strong-point detonated by United States Marines. Below American troops are seen encircling a pillbox.

ALLIES REACH CASSINO. On 11 and 12 February in spite of very bad weather the fighting continued with increasing ferocity in the suburbs of Cassino and on the slopes of the mountain. An enemy strong-point in the basement of the town prison was wiped out and the shell of the building occupied. An important 1,500 ft. height two miles to the west was also captured. Above, a column of German soldiers file away. Top right, Italian peasants point out mines and booby traps to Allied soldiers. Bottom right, peasants return home after Germans have left.

R.A.F. OVER BERLIN. On 15 February the R.A.F. made a very large scale night attack on Berlin. Over 1,000 aircraft dropped 2,500 tons of bombs at the rate of eighty tons a minute. The ground defences were active but little fighter opposition was met. Large fires were started and the smoke clouds rose four miles high. The communications of the city were put out of action. Top left, Allied bombers on a raid over Europe. Bottom left, incendiary bombs drop towards their target. Above, high-explosive bombs drop on a Nazi rail centre.

CLEARING THE NGAKYEDYANK PASS. In Burma in mid-February the Allies were fighting for the control of the Ngakyedyank Pass on the Arakan front. On 19 February the S.E. Asia Command announced that "in the last forty-eight hours the main Japanese force on the Arakan front has been showing signs of becoming unco-ordinated in face of continuous determined fighting and growing pressure by our troops." On 21 February the 14th Army recaptured an important height (Point 1070) which overlooked the west end of the Ngakyedyank

Pass and three days later the road through the pass was again being used by the Allies. A British convoy, supported by tanks, was able to pass through to relieve the 7th Indian Division. A series of Japanese counter-attacks were repulsed and severe casualties inflicted on the enemy. The next day Allied traffic was passing through unmolested although Japanese troops were still holding out at the north end of the pass. A few days later the Japanese were in full retreat. Picture shows U.S. engineers passing down China's new Burma Road.

U.S. ATTACK ON MARIANA ISLANDS. On 22 February the first Allied attacks were launched on the Mariana Islands. The force consisted of some hundreds of carrier-based aircraft of the U.S. Pacific Fleet which attacked Saipan and Tinian Islands. They were able to make two effective attacks and cause very considerable damage. A further naval attack supported by aircraft was made on Guam, a one-time American base which fell into Japanese hands in December, 1941. The force was detected before its arrival near the

target and was subjected to a concentrated bombing attack by Japanese bombers and torpedo-carrying aircraft. The American force succeeded, however, in sinking a cargo ship and a patrol vessel and seriously damaged two other cargo ships and seven other small vessels. The aerodrome received direct hits. The Japanese lost 135 aircraft, of which eighty-seven were destroyed on the ground, thirty-four in combat and fourteen by warships' A.A. fire. The picture shows the burning hangar installations on the airstrip on the island of Tinian.

ADVANCING ON MOGAUNG. In mid-March Sino-American troops had completely cleared the enemy from the Hukawng Valley and were attacking the Jumbubum Pass, which was its southern exit. On 20 March this was captured. The Chinese 22nd Division entered the Mogaung valley two days later and was fighting between Jumbubum and Shaduzup, only about forty-five miles from Mogaung itself. On 25 March Shaduzup fell and the Chinese continued to advance on Mogaung. Above, Chinese troops carrying supplies on the march in Burma.

FRESH LANDINGS IN NEW GUINEA. On 5 March the Americans made a further landing on New Guinea at Mundiri, covered by strong naval and air support, and captured the Yalan Plantation, where a small enemy force was trapped. By 9 March they controlled thirty-five miles of the coast. Meanwhile the Australians, who were advancing along the coast, captured the village of Daumonia and other places in the Mintjim Valley. This placed them on the motor-road leading to Bogadjim. Above, troops on a landing-craft off New Guinea rest on trucks.

JUNGLE-FIGHTING IN BURMA. In early March a large Japanese force was trapped between Mainkwang and Walawbum. On 11 March Lieutenant-General Stilwell's G.H.Q. announced that Sino-American forces were within sixty miles of the Mandalay-Myitkyina Railway and that mopping-up operations were being carried out against the 18th Division and that 2,000 Japanese had been killed. The Chinese 22nd and 38th Divisions had linked up in the Walawbum area. On 12 March an advance of three miles south of Walawbum was made and the Chinese 22nd Division crossed the Nampuyk River and captured the village of Lalawng. They cut the only motor-road leading to Kamaing and were only a few miles from the pass leading out of the valley. Above, a Japanese train carrying oil on fire after being attacked by R.A.F. "Beaufighters" on the Rangoon-Mandalay Railway. Left, a single shot from the powerful cannon of an Allied bomber blows up a half-million gallon oil tank in Burma.

OCCUPATION OF MANUS ISLAND. On 15 March, American troops landed on Manus Island in the Admiralty group after a heavy preliminary bombardment from the sea and from the air. The first attack destroyed land-mines, machine gun nests and booby traps and advanced inland in the Lorengau airfield. On the following day, the airfield was captured and the Americans were only 600 yards from Lorenhau itself. On 18 March after a very fierce tank battle at close quarters Lorengau fell. Support was given from the sea by U.S. destroyers. A large number of the garrison was killed and the remainder fled into the hills. Very much equipment and many supplies were taken. Top left, American troops, holding their weapons and ammunition above level of the waters ford a river. Bottom left, the Allies land supplies on Green Island. A landing-craft may be seen behind. Above, American marines watch intently as the Japanese are blasted out of strong-points on one of the islands taken.

ATTACK ON CASSINO. On 17 March heavy fighting was in progress in the ruins of Cassino. New Zealand troops succeeded in capturing the railway station and its loss was admitted by the enemy who later bombed it from the air. On either side of Cassino, Indian troops were engaged in fierce hill fighting. Above, a tank commander, wounded by a German sniper, receives medical aid. Right, a German propaganda photograph shows German soldiers cross-examining peasants about some hand-grenades which were found in the straw behind their hut.

ALLIED AIR ACTIVITY IN EUROPE. While the Allies were advancing in Italy, enemy targets and communications were being relentlessly harried from the air.   On 17 March the M.A.A.F. flew over 1,600 sorties bombing supply dumps on the Anzio and Cassino fronts. On 20 March they flew 1,100 sorties in spite of bad weather and attacked rail targets at Terni, Poggibonsi and Orvieto.   Enemy ports at San Stefano, Piombino and Porto Ercoe were also attacked. In these sorties, six enemy aircraft were destroyed for the loss of only three. The following day, 800 sorties were flown in spite of continuing bad conditions. The targets included rail yards in Rome and Florence, viaducts in Arezzo and Bucini and a bridge at Tarquinia, besides enemy road traffic and gun-positions. Four machines were lost. Left, waves of "Liberators" attack the Concordia oil refinery at Ploesti. Heavy flak is visible near the machines. Above, enemy vehicles destroyed and damaged in the Rome area by Allied Air Forces.

131

ALLIES OVER OCCUPIED FRANCE

In Western Europe, the Allied Air Forces continued to make devastating attacks on enemy targets both by day and by night. On 22 March, for instance, about 600 8th U.S.A.A.F. "Fortresses" and "Liberators" escorted by between 750 and 1,000 "Mustangs," "Thunderbolts" and "Lightnings" made a heavy daylight attack on Berlin and dropped about 1,400 tons of bombs. Next day 1,750 American bombers and fighters attacked industrial targets including the Hamm rail yards, Luftwaffe bases at Achmer (near Osnabruck), Handorf (near Munster), and a Messerschmitt production centre at Brunswick. Rail centres at Creil, Haine St. Pierre, and airfields a Beaumont-Le-Roger and Beauvais Tille were also attacked. At night, the R.A.F. attacked targets a Laon, Lyons and Dortmund. Top, bridges over Seine wrecked by R.A.F. Below: left, American bombers attacking German base at Avord, near Bourges; right, attack on German airfield at Montpellier.

ON THE ANZIO BEACHHEAD

24-27 MARCH, 1944

Meanwhile the slow progress on the Anzio beachhead had been causing considerable anxiety in some quarters although the official report had stated that the situation was "well in hand." The Germans continued to launch heavy attacks with great frequency and on 24 March they resorted again to long-range shelling. There were several sharp artillery duels and although two strong enemy patrols were destroyed while attempting to filter through the Allied lines, bad weather conditions prevented very much patrolling activity on either side. There was considerable aerial activity over the Anzio front. "Warhawks" and "Thunderbolts" attacked enemy gun positions, ammunition dumps and other targets. Strong Luftwaffe opposition was met. On 27 March five enemy machines were destroyed when the enemy made an unsuccessful raid on the port of Anzio. There were no Allied losses. The next day the Germans made a further attack and bombed two hospitals. The casualties amounted to eight killed and seventy wounded. But in the meantime the enemy were unable to prevent the steady flow of war materials coming into the beachhead and ships continued to arrive at Anzio harbour in spite of attacks by U-boats, fighter-bombers and radio-controlled glider bombers. Owing to the extensive demolitions around the harbour, supply ships had to anchor off-shore and unload their cargoes on to ducks and landing-craft. The picture shows the inner harbour of Anzio where two landing craft are unloading. In the background can be seen some of the buildings damaged by heavy shell fire and aerial bombardment.

KAMENETS-PODOLSKI CAPTURED. On 25 March Marshal Zhukov captured Proskurov, a junction on the Lwow-Odessa line. Meanwhile other troops of his army were fighting in Kamenets-Podolski and were driving on to Zalesezyk. On the following day Kamenets-Podolski fell to the Red Army, which meant that the Germans in the salient north of the Dniester had all their road and rail routes cut off and were left with no chance of escape other than by crossing the river. On 27 March the towns of Gorodenlea and Zastavna were captured and the city of Cernauti, capital of the province of Bukovina, was threatened with encirclement. On 29 March Marshal Zhukov entered the suburbs of Cernauti trapping the German forces north of the Dniester. Above, German troops retreat through driving snow and ankle deep in mud. Top left, a Red Army anti-tank gun in action. Bottom left, wounded and exhausted German soldiers crowd on a mud-encrusted armoured car which moves with difficulty.

137

SMALL SHIPS IN ACTION

On 29 March there was considerable activity on the seas of Western Europe. Light coastal forces fought an action two miles from Dieppe when they attacked a convoy of three small enemy boats escorted by four R-boats and some larger escort vessels. An R-boat was seriously damaged and later a loud explosion was heard from the enemy convoy. All the boats of the attacking force returned safely having suffered only minor casualties. Another force of "small" ships attacked a convoy escorted by R-boats near Ymunden in Holland. In the ensuing action, several enemy ships were severely damaged while the Allied force suffered no casualties. In this action, the crews of the British M.T.B.s went in with the cutlasses and clubs which the vessels always carry. Later that day, a large German convoy was attacked by "Beau-fighters" of the R.A.F. Coastal Command near the Frisian Islands off North Germany and two heavily laden cargo ships were hit by torpedoes. All five of the escort vessels and three other ships were severely damaged by cannon fire. In these actions, the Germans claimed that the British lost ten ships while another ten were alleged to be seriously damaged. In actual fact, no British vessels were sunk at all during the course of the actions. Enemy shipping losses on the other hand were heavy and M.T.B.s and other "small ships" accounted for many of these. For instance, five British sloops, "Starling," "Wild Goose," "Woodpecker," "Kite," and "Magpie" set up a record by sinking six enemy U-boats during a German attack on an Atlantic convoy. The picture on the left shows "Beaufighters" of the R.A.F. Coastal Command attacking the German convoy on 29 March. Smoke is seen rising from a 3,000-ton enemy merchant ship which has just been raked by cannon fire.

GERMAN ATROCITIES. On 30 March Marshal Stalin was able to announce that Cernauti, capital of Bukovina, was in Russian hands. Huge quantities of rolling-stock and stores were captured and on the following day a rapid advance brought the 1st Ukrainian Army within fifteen miles of the borders of Czechoslovakia. Other troops, under Marshal Zhukov's command advanced to the upper reaches of the River Sereth and were fighting outside Soviet territory. The two Rumanian towns of Darbani and Mamaliga were captured. Above, Nazi soldiers execute Russian peasants. Top left, the body of a Russian working girl hanging in a Ukrainian town. Bottom left, whole families of dead Russians, murdered by the Nazis, lie outside the ruin of a building that was once their home.

ALLIED AIR FORCES IN BURMA. During the advances of March and April one of the many duties of the Allied Air Forces was to keep the troops in forward areas fully supplied with everything necessary to them. Sometimes supplies were landed by parachute, but in other cases actual landings were made under difficult conditions, so that the sick and wounded could be evacuated on the return journey. In addition a constant struggle was being maintained against enemy communications. Top left, supplies being dropped in Burma by parachute. Bottom left, phosphorus bombs are dropped on a Japanese airfield. The value of these bombs is being increasingly realized and it is the job of the Chemical Warfare Service to supply them. The manufacture of these constitutes half of its work and it now turns out seven main types. Above, U.S. aircraft, belonging to the First Air Commando Force, which operated with the late Major-General Wingate's expedition in Burma, take off from an airfield.

RED ARMY IN TARNOPOL. By 1 April the German News Agency admitted that Marshal Zhukov's 1st Ukrainian Army had reached the Yablonica Pass and that Tarnopol and Brody had been cut off. Indeed the greater part of Tarnopol was now in Russian hands and it was estimated that there were over 3,000 casualties in the fierce street fighting in that city. Next day, Kosov and Kuty on the borders of Poland and Bukovina were taken and on 3 April, Gorokhov, Berestechko and Lopatin fell. The Red Army was now only forty miles from Lwow. In the Skala pocket,

many trapped divisions were being destroyed and enemy attempts to relieve them were broken. Khotin was taken on the same day and the garrison destroyed. Rapid progress was made in the direction of Kishinev against fierce resistance. On this, as on other fronts, the German retreat was fast becoming a rout. Top, German tanks set fire to a Russian village. Left, shows all that remains of a German tank column after an attack by Soviet aircraft. Right, a scene in a Ukrainian village during a German retreat. Enemy dead may be seen littering the streets.

ATTACK ON THE "TIRPITZ." On 3 April a force of "Barracudas" from a British aircraft carrier made two very successful attacks on the German battleship "Tirpitz" in Altenfjord, where she was undergoing repairs after being torpedoed by British midget submarines. The first force of bombers scored hits near the bridge and the second on the after-turret, amidships and on the forecastle. Violent explosions were heard and flames were seen as high as the mainmast. The damage was severe enought to put the "Tirpitz" out of action for many months. Top left, "Barracuda" bombers approach Altenfjord. Bottom left and above, the attack on the "Tirpitz."

TRANSPORT IN BURMA. One of the main difficulties in the Burma campaign was ground transport. Jeep tracks had to be hacked through jungles hitherto regarded as impassable and roads built over mountains in the Assam area. Very considerable use was made of pack animals, and in rivers where boats were not available, rafts were built. Hastily prepared ground strips had to be cleared to accommodate aircraft. Top left, U.S. troops load their pack animals before starting on the march. Bottom left, Allied troops clear a landing strip so that the troop transports of General Wingate can land. The troops engaged on this clearance work were landed by gliders. Above, a part of the newly built highway between Imphal and Ukhral connecting up with the 14th Army in Assam.

IMPERIAL CONFERENCE

In early May the four Dominion Premiers visited London for the Imperial Conference to discuss the war and peace policies of their united peoples. Pictures show: top, Mr. Mackenzie King addresses Parliament (reproduced by permission of "The Times"); bottom left, Mr. Curtin receives the Freedom of the City at Guildhall; below, before the opening of the conference. Left to right: front row, Mr. Attlee (Deputy Prime Minister), Mr. Frazer (New Zealand), Mr. Mackenzie King (Canada), Mr. Churchill, Mr. Curtin (Australia), Field Marshal Smuts (South Africa), Mr. Eden; back row, Lord Woolton (Minister of Reconstruction), Mr. Oliver Lyttleton (Minister of Production), Sir John Anderson (Chancellor of the Exchequer), Mr. Ernest Bevin (Minister of Labour) and Mr. Herbert Morrison (Home Secretary).

FIGHT FOR MYITKYINA. On 26 May the Allies succeeded in cutting off Myitkyina, and two days later very heavy fighting was in progress round the town. Toward evening, Chinese and American troops succeeded in entering its outer suburbs. Meanwhile, Allied artillery heavily bombarded enemy transport in the northern area, and enemy attempts to relieve the garrison were repulsed with many casualties. On 29 May the Allies advanced 600 yards into the town, beating down fierce enemy resistance every yard of the way and repulsing a powerful counter-attack. Hand-to-hand fighting continued all the next day, and to the south of the town the "Chindits" prevented enemy attempts at relief by attacking enemy communications. On 31 May the attack continued with unabated fury under strong air cover and many Japanese pillboxes and entrenchments were overcome. By the following day, half the town was in enemy hands and Sino-American troops continued systematically to dislodge the Japanese from dug-outs and pillboxes with the help of Allied Air Forces. Above, Allied troops making a trackway in Burma. Top right, bombing a railway bridge. Below right, crossing a bridge.

FALL OF ROME

By 3 June the Americans were only ten miles from Rome and the enemy was falling back rapidly, although still maintaining good order. The Germans lost great quantities of equipment, however, largely owing to skilful and accurate bombing by the Tactical Air Force, and the Campo Leone area was described as being "littered with enemy tanks and vehicles." Several German convoys had been caught falling back north and some hundreds of vehicles had been destroyed. Owing to the rapidity of their retreat, the Germans were unable to carry out demolitions. By evening the whole of Highway 6 to within a few miles of Rome had been cleared of the enemy. At 7.15 next morning American troops had reached the outskirts of Rome where they engaged German rearguards. By 9.15 Allied tanks entered the city and by evening Rome had been liberated. Top left, General Mark Clark talks to a Roman priest near the Vatican. Bottom left, Allied soldiers wave to the crowd from Mussolini's famous balcony. Right, the liberators pass the Colosseum.

D-DAY

6 JUNE, 1944

A little before midnight on 5 June Allied bombers made a heavy attack on the Normandy coast. These assaults in very great strength lasted until shortly before dawn. Early next morning two naval task forces under Rear-Admiral Sir Philip Vian and Rear-Admiral Alan Kirke successfully landed on the enemy beaches. These forces were under the supreme command of Admiral Sir Bertram Ramsay and were joined by the bombarding forces in the course of the night. Landing operations were successfully completed shortly before dawn. Enemy torpedo boats which attempted to interfere were successfully driven off, and one of their number was sunk and another severely damaged. Assault troops were landed under heavy fire from destroyers while battleships engaged enemy shore batteries. Further troops were landed by gliders and troop-carrying machines. The beaches were covered by intensive cross-fire from German pillboxes, but although the casualties were not light, they were not nearly so heavy as had been expected. Underwater obstacles were encountered neck deep by commandos who came first ashore, but in spite of these difficulties, they succeeded in landing and silencing the pillboxes. Meanwhile Allied fighter bombers continued to attack the beaches in very great strength, attacking gun emplacements, defensive works and communications. Continuous fighter cover was also given over the naval operations, the beaches and even some miles inland. Night fighters protected the transports. On the first day, penetrations of several miles inland were made. The enemy was completely taken by surprise and important bridges were seized before the Germans had time to demolish them. The picture, reproduced by permission of the Netherlands Government Information Bureau, shows Dutch troops of the "Princess Irene" Brigade landing on the beaches of Normandy.

LANDINGS IN NORMANDY. Meanwhile very powerful naval and air support continued to protect the fresh troops and supplies which were continuously poured on to the Normandy beaches. Minefields were kept clear by 10,000 officers and men using 2,800 tons of minesweeping gear and nearly seventy miles of minesweeping wire. German coastal batteries were bombarded by 640 naval guns from all types of craft. The shelling very often took place at close range and land forces often completed the work of knocking out enemy strong-posts. At

the same time the Allied air forces kept up the offensive at a maximum scale. Early in the day 1,300 "Liberators" and "Fortresses" heavily bombed over 100 German coastal strong-points. No opposition was met with. Later in the day more U.S machines made attacks on targets farther inland, but some of them had to bring back their bomb loads on account of poor visibility. Then at night the R.A.F. sent out 1,000 machines to attack bridges and road communications behind enemy lines. The drawing by C. E. Turner shows the landing in Normandy.

CLEARING THE BEACHES OF NORMANDY

On the evening of 6 June fighting was in progress in the old Norman town of Caen, and penetrations had reached a depth of ten miles at several points between Havre and Cherbourg. A strong German armoured counter-attack in the neighbourhood of Caen was repulsed. Meanwhile over 4,000 ships of all types with thousands of smaller vessels were landing fresh troops under strong air cover. Minefields were kept clear by 200 minesweepers. The following day, the enemy were completely driven from the beaches and seaborne and airborne troops had linked up. Top, Allied infantry wade ashore. Bottom left, a landing craft approaches the beach. Bottom right, assault troops disembark from a landing craft in Normandy.

CAPTURE OF CIVITA VECCHIA. On 7 June, the Germans were falling rapidly back from Rome, hotly pursued by the Allies. All the Roman airfields had been lost by the enemy. Very little resistance was met with from what remained of the German Tenth and Fourteenth Armies. Prisoners from as many as forty different forma-tions which had become completely isolated were taken. In the hospitals of Rome, 8,000 wounded had been captured. That same day, Civita Vecchia, an important port and naval base, was captured. Meanwhile, many reports were received of increasing disorders among Kesselring's troops. Next day, Allied troops pushed up beyond Civita Vecchia; and Civita Castellana, Caprarola and Sutri were all captured. Top left, wrecked ships in the harbour of Civita Vecchia as a result of Allied bombing and German demolitions. Bottom left, Allied troops and tanks move through wrecked town. Above, French machine gunners move to new post in demolished street.

ATTACK ON CAEN. On 7 June, Bayeux was captured by General Montgomery's troops and the Caen-Bayeux road crossed at several points. Bayeux fell after little fighting and was left more or less undamaged. The liberating troops were given a very warm reception by the local people. The next day, two important bridges just north of Caen were seized and held in the face of determined counter-attacks. By 9 June, fierce fighting was in progress for Caen itself. This continued throughout all the next day and many armoured counter-attacks were beaten off by the British and Canadians. The German 21st Panzer Division and 176th Infantry were holding Caen with grim

determination and anti-tank ditches and strong defences were being hastily thrown up to try and stem the Allied advance. Fierce panzer attacks were made along the line of the Caen canal and Orne estuary which was successfully held by the 6th Airborne Division. On 13 June, Caen, which had already been severely damaged by constant artillery bombardment, was subjected to heavy shelling by the guns of Allied battleships. The vessels which made this attack in support of the ground forces were H.M.S. "Nelson" and H.M.S. "Ramillies." The reconnaissance photograph on these pages shows big fires burning in various parts of the city after the shelling ceased.

ALLIED PROBLEMS IN NORMANDY. Although the Normandy landings were achieved more easily than had been expected, the operation was not smooth going all the way owing to a variety of reasons. The weather was extremely bad and the defences wh ch had to be overcome under these d fficult circumstances were in great depth. It was only the profound knowledge of the d fficulties to be encountered, ogether with careful planning and magnificent organization as well as air and sea superiority, which overcame them A few of the Allied orders

were captured by the Germans, and their comments upon them show that they were astonished by the thoroughness of all preparations. Owing to this element of surprise, the initial break-through was very speedy. Bayeux was captured comparatively easily, and in a few days the Allies were twenty miles inland. At this point, Allied progress inevitably slowed down except for an advance by the Americans across the Cotentin Peninsula in an attempt to isolate the whole region. Picture shows landing of French 2nd Armoured Division in Normandy.

TRUK RAIDED. On 29 and 30 April, a large American force under Vice-Admiral Mark A. Mitscher, consisting of battleships, aircraft-carriers, cruisers and destroyers, made a heavy attack on the Japanese naval base at Truk. Carrier-based aircraft dropped 800 tons of bombs on ground installations, which were very severely damaged. Japanese losses were very heavy, 126 machines being destroyed in the aerial fighting, while the Allies escaped very lightly, losing only about 30 flight personnel. Not a single American ship was damaged. Mr.

Forrestal, U.S. Navy Secretary in Washington, stated that in this attack on Truk, together with those on Saipan, Tinian and Palau, the enemy lost 500 aircraft and 52 warships and merchant ships, while 32 more were damaged. American losses consisted of only 48 aircraft. Truk was again raided on 2 and 3 June, when 3 destroyers and 17 interceptor aeroplanes were destroyed for the loss of only 1 Allied machine. A further attack was made on the base on 11 and 12 June, when 38 tons of bombs were dropped. The photograph shows the attack on Truk.

FURTHER ADVANCES
IN NORMANDY

On 13 June, Allied positions were very greatly improved. On this day Montebourg, Le Ham, Pont l'Abbé and Villers Bocage were captured. Very heavy fighting continued round Caen, and the Allies threatened to outflank the city. Between Caen and Tilly a huge tank battle was raging. On 14 June, a British thrust captured the village of Caumont, 1,000 feet above sea level and commanding all the surrounding countryside. The next day the Americans were forced to give up the now ruined town of Montebourg, but pressed forward on either side of it for some miles and took the small fishing village of Quineville. Reigneville and Baupté were also captured. Fierce enemy attacks were made on the village of Caumont which successfully held out. On 17 June, the last enemy coastal stronghold, Douves, was captured by Royal Marine Commandos. They suffered only one casualty and took 150 prisoners. Next day Barneville-sur-Mer was captured, thus cutting off Cherbourg. The German 77th Division launched desperate counter-attacks in an attempt to break out of the trap, but these were repelled with heavy losses both in men and materials. On 19 June the Americans were within eight miles of Cherbourg which was being heavily shelled. Montebourg was recaptured together with a dozen villages. Later in the day Tilly and Hattot were captured after hand-to-hand fighting in drenching rain. Many prisoners were taken. The picture on these pages shows a gun crew of the Royal Artillery in action.

FLYING BOMBS OVER ENGLAND

In mid June, the German High Command issued a communique devoted to the flying bomb. It was claimed that it was "the beginning of the day of vengeance." The Berlin radio had announced that Kingston, Bromley, Sevenoaks, Sutton, Southampton and the Daventry radio station had all been severely hit and that the whole of Southern England was covered by dense smoke clouds over a huge area. It was also stated that in the capital, warehouses and docks were ablaze and the whole railway system paralysed. These reports were grossly exaggerated, true to Nazi form. Above, a flying bomb passes over a residential area. Left, a flying bomb seen just before it crashed in Southern England. Right, ruins of the Guards' Chapel at Wellington Barracks after it had been gutted by a flying bomb.

GERMANY'S V.1. During the month of June, 1944, Southern England suffered many blows from the flying bomb, a weapon of pure reprisal and of little military value. Once launched, it could not be directed with any accuracy and therefore could not be aimed at any specific target. First news of the flying bomb had been heard in April, 1943, when reports were received that the Germans were developing a new type of long-range weapon. In November, it was discovered that the enemy were building flying-bomb sites all along the French coast from

Cherbourg to Calais, almost all oriented in the direction of London. Throughout December, the Allied Air Forces had systematically attacked and annihilated them in spite of much camouflage. As the enemy rebuilt them, they were again destroyed. During the early days of the attacks, 1,000 flying bombs were destroyed by fighters, and perpetual patrols were maintained over the English Channel. The picture shows damage caused by a flying bomb which fell in Aldwych, London. The wreckage of an omnibus may be seen in the foreground.

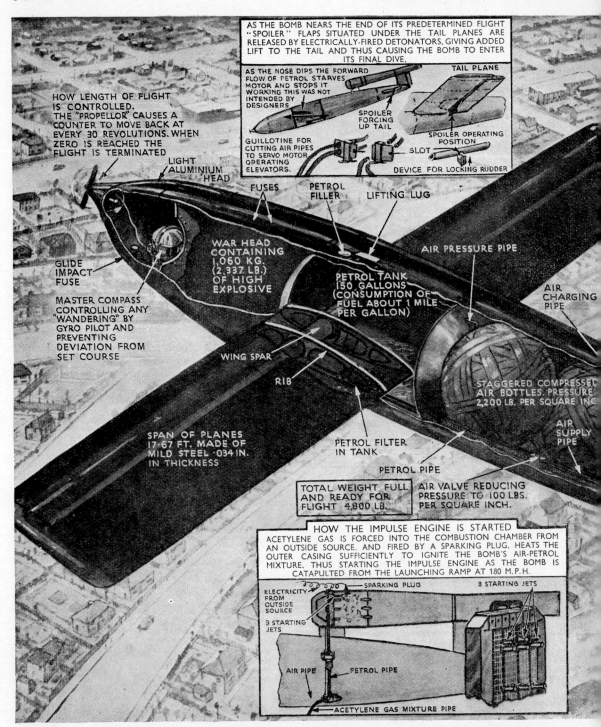

GERMAN FLYING BOMB. This is a small automatic, steel-constructed aircraft, easily produced in quantity. The power unit consists of a thin metal tube, open at the rear but closed at the front by a grille containing several shutters. On the launching ramp, acetylene gas is fed to the tube from outside and is ignited by a sparking plug. The mixture heats the tube and the bomb is then catapulted off at 180 m.p.h. bringing the impulse motor into action (see lower and top right-hand insets). The aiming of the bomb is achieved by pre-setting the automatic

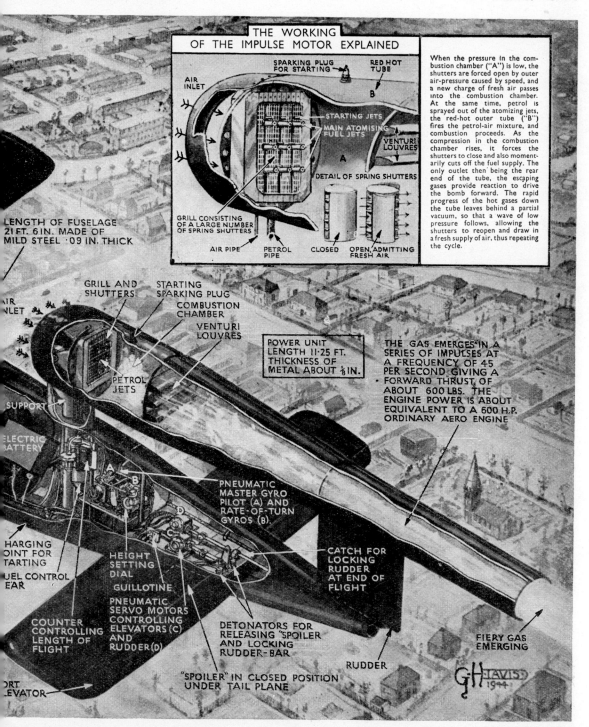

THE WORKING
OF THE IMPULSE MOTOR EXPLAINED

SPARKING PLUG
FOR STARTING

RED HOT
TUBE

B

AIR
INLET

STARTING JETS

MAIN ATOMISING
FUEL JETS

VENTURI
LOUVRES

A

DETAIL OF SPRING SHUTTERS

GRILL CONSISTING
OF A LARGE NUMBER
OF SPRING SHUTTERS

AIR PIPE   PETROL   CLOSED   OPEN, ADMITTING
              PIPE   FRESH AIR

When the pressure in the combustion chamber ("A") is low, the shutters are forced open by outer air-pressure caused by speed, and a new charge of fresh air passes into the combustion chamber. At the same time, petrol is sprayed out of the atomizing jets, the red-hot outer tube ("B") fires the petrol-air mixture, and combustion proceeds. As the compression in the combustion chamber rises, it forces the shutters to close and also momentarily cuts off the fuel supply. The only outlet then being the rear end of the tube, the escaping gases provide reaction to drive the bomb forward. The rapid progress of the hot gases down the tube leaves behind a partial vacuum, so that a wave of low pressure follows, allowing the shutters to reopen and draw in a fresh supply of air, thus repeating the cycle.

LENGTH OF FUSELAGE
21 FT. 6 IN. MADE OF
MILD STEEL ·09 IN. THICK

GRILL AND
SHUTTERS

STARTING
SPARKING PLUG

COMBUSTION
CHAMBER

VENTURI
LOUVRES

AIR
INLET

POWER UNIT
LENGTH 11·25 FT.
THICKNESS OF
METAL ABOUT ⅛ IN.

THE GAS EMERGES IN A
SERIES OF IMPULSES AT
A FREQUENCY OF 45
PER SECOND GIVING A
FORWARD THRUST OF
ABOUT 600 LBS. THE
ENGINE POWER IS ABOUT
EQUIVALENT TO A 600 H.P.
ORDINARY AERO ENGINE

PETROL
JETS

SUPPORT

ELECTRIC
BATTERY

PNEUMATIC
MASTER GYRO
PILOT (A) AND
RATE-OF-TURN
GYROS (B).

CHARGING
POINT FOR
STARTING

FUEL CONTROL
GEAR

HEIGHT
SETTING
DIAL

GUILLOTINE

PNEUMATIC
SERVO MOTORS
CONTROLLING
ELEVATORS (C)
AND
RUDDER (D)

CATCH FOR
LOCKING
RUDDER
AT END OF
FLIGHT

COUNTER
CONTROLLING
LENGTH OF
FLIGHT

DETONATORS FOR
RELEASING "SPOILER
AND LOCKING
RUDDER-BAR

"SPOILER" IN CLOSED POSITION
UNDER TAIL PLANE

RUDDER

FIERY GAS
EMERGING

PORT
ELEVATOR

G H DAVIS
1944

pilot, a gyroscope driven by compressed air: the height of travel is also pre-set and is controlled by an aerial barometer. A small airscrew in the nose drives a shaft whose revolutions are counted, measuring off exactly the chosen range. When this point is reached, the bomb is pushed into its final dive by the use of electrically fired detonators, which release "spoiler" flaps situated in the tail planes and so lift the rear of the robot (see top left-hand inset). This drawing by G. H. Davis is reproduced here by courtesy of the "Illustrated London News."

WAR OF MOVEMENT IN NORMANDY

The Allied sweep across the Cherbourg Peninsula left a train of devastation behind it. By 18 June, American troops under General Omar Bradley had succeeded in completely cutting off the Cherbourg Peninsula, reaching Cape Cartevet and Barneville on the west coast and thus trapping an enemy force of 25,000 men. Meanwhile Cherbourg itself was in the gravest danger. The Allied navies had hemmed in the garrison from the sea while their big guns continuously battered the fortifications of the port, and small ships prevented an escape by water. In spite of the hopeless situation, the German High Command was determined to hold the port of Cherbourg at all costs, the object being to hold Allied troops in the area in the hope that reinforcements could ultimately be brought up in sufficient numbers to launch a counter-offensive. The picture shows French civilian refugees at Pont l'Abbé passing an overturned war vehicle with a dead German lying beside it. The village of Pont l'Abbé was turned into a strong-point by the enemy and therefore suffered very considerable damage before the Americans could eject them in their advance on Cherbourg.

FRENCH LEADER IN BAYEUX.   On 20 June, the Americans made a rapid advance towards Cherbourg without meeting serious opposition, and by the evening were in St. Martin in the outer defences and only four miles from the port.   A few days earlier General de Gaulle had arrived in Normandy to visit a number of places which had been liberated by the Anglo-American forces. Top left, General de Gaulle addresses a crowd. Bottom left, the people of Bayeux await his arrival. Above, General de Gaulle walks through the streets of Bayeux.

IN THE CHERBOURG REGION.   On 21 June, the Americans under Lieutenant-General Omar Bradley were fighting only three miles from Cherbourg.   Allied broadcasts were sent to the workers of Cherbourg asking them to prevent docks, railways and factories being destroyed by the enemy.   Left, Mr. Churchill, General Smuts, General Montgomery and Field Marshal Sir A. Brooke, Chief of the Imperial General Staff, watch an air battle in the Cherbourg Peninsula.   Above, Mr. Churchill visits a captured flying-bomb site in the area.

CHERBOURG SURROUNDED. On 22 June, an intense air and artillery attack was made on Cherbourg. The aerial attack lasted for eighty minutes and waves of light and medium bombers flying at 100 feet blasted German strong positions and pillboxes. At 2 p.m. the infantry attacked. By evening the city was almost surrounded and the capture of St. Pierre Eglise cut the coastal highway and rendered the isolation more complete. The road leading to Cape de la Hague was also cut. Top left, German prisoners pass into captivity. Bottom left, American vehicles press forward along the banks of a stream. Above, tanks explode mines to make a path for the infantry. The use of armoured vehicles for clearing mines is a great improvement on the method of lifting them by infantry.

185

FINAL ASSAULT ON CHERBOURG. The fierce fighting for Cherbourg continued throughout 23 June. The Americans captured the hill position of Tourlaville which overlooks the city and is only a mile from the harbour. By the evening of 24 June, after very severe hand-to-hand fighting amid enemy pillboxes and barbed-wire defences, the Americans were only 2,000 yards from the harbour. The following day they advanced to within a few hundred yards of the harbour and the Germans could be seen carrying out demolitions and blowing up ammunition dumps and lorries. Top left, U.S. engineers demolish buildings. Bottom left, an anti-tank gun crew in action. Above an Allied vehicle outside a village receives a direct hit by a German shell and is set on fire.

CHERBOURG
CAPTURED

On 26 June American troops reached the waterfront at Cherbourg and so split the German garrison. The Germans had turned the arsenal into a strong-point and it was assaulted by the Americans with bayonets and hand grenades. A number of pillboxes and strong-points in the outer suburbs of the city still held out and these were by-passed by the Americans. The garrison, 300 strong, of a subterranean fort 200 feet underground, surrendered. Three thousand prisoners were taken. Next day, the group holding out in the arsenal surrendered and the fall of Cherbourg was announced. The enemy lost four divisions and Lieutenant-General Carl von Schlieben, commander of the garrison, and Rear-Admiral Hennecke, naval commander of the Normandy defences, were among the captured. Top, Cherbourg docks with fires raging. Bottom left, Lieutenant-General Schlieben and Rear-Admiral Hennecke immediately after they had surrendered. Below, German prisoners are hurried to captivity.

IN A BATTLE-SCARRED VILLAGE. On 29 June, two days after the fall of the port itself was announced, a number of enemy batteries in the Cherbourg Peninsula were still holding out at Querqueville and round Cape de la Hague. Among these was the island fort of Port de l'Ile Pelee, which surrendered to the Americans on 30 June. The rest were finally overcome on 2 July and about 2,000 prisoners were taken. Some enemy troops who had attempted a sea-borne evacuation from Cape de la Hague were destroyed by the American air forces,

and their vessels sunk. Several large railway guns were amongst the considerable amount of German equipment which was captured in the peninsula. With the end of the enemy resistance in the Cherbourg Peninsula, two large Luftwaffe air bases fell into Allied hands—the Maupertus and Querqueville airfields. Messages of congratulation on the liberation of Cherbourg were sent to Mr. Churchill and President Roosevelt by Marshal Stalin. The picture on these pages shows an Allied tank advancing through the ruined streets of a much-battered village.

MINSK CAPTURED. On 23 June, the Red Army launched a great offensive which advanced 250 miles in three weeks. On 26 June, Vitebsk fell, Minsk was seriously threatened and Mogilev stormed. Next day Bobruisk was taken. In these operations the Germans lost 80,000 dead in addition to wounded and prisoners of war. On 3 July, Minsk was captured after having been in German hands for three years. Next day the important rail junction of Polotsk was captured. On 7 July the Russians had extended to a 400-mile front and by 10 July they

were fighting in the streets of Vilna and had reached the Latvian border. That same day, Lida was captured and the Russians were within seventy miles of the border of East Prussia. Major Schafer, Military Correspondent of the "Berliner Boersenzeitung" said: "The extremely heavy battles have inflicted distressing losses on the German side. No one among us can gloss this over." The picture shows citizens of Minsk with their furniture and various belongings, outside their burning homes which were set on fire by the Germans before their retreat.

ALLIES BREAK OUT OF THE BRIDGEHEAD

2 JULY—4 AUGUST, 1944

On 2 July, the greater part of the Cherbourg Peninsula being in Allied hands, repair work in the city was going on rapidly. Four forts in the dock area were the last to surrender, but these were effectively bombed by "Marauders" from 6,000 feet and pounded to surrender. So accurate was the bombing that although the forts were severely damaged, the whole length of the breakwater on which they were situated was only superficially blasted. What damage there was, was largely the result of German demolitions. By 5 July, steady progress was being made across the base of the Cherbourg Peninsula on a thirteen-and-a-half-mile sector which took the Allies to the top of the 400-ft. hills about three miles north of the road junction of La Haye de Puits, a remarkable advance in view of the wooded and marshy country which particularly favoured the defensive tactics of the enemy. On 6 July, very great advances were made. The right wing thrust farther down to the west coast and another column struck down the Carentan-Periers road. By 7 July, the road was successfully cut a mile south of La Haye, and the village of Blemont was captured. The map by S. J. Turner, F.R.G.S., illustrates the campaign in the Cherbourg Peninsula and shows the breakthrough into Brittany on 4 August.

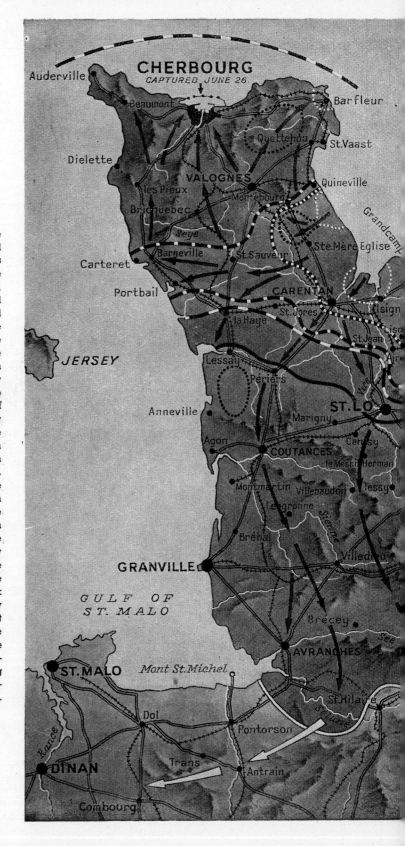

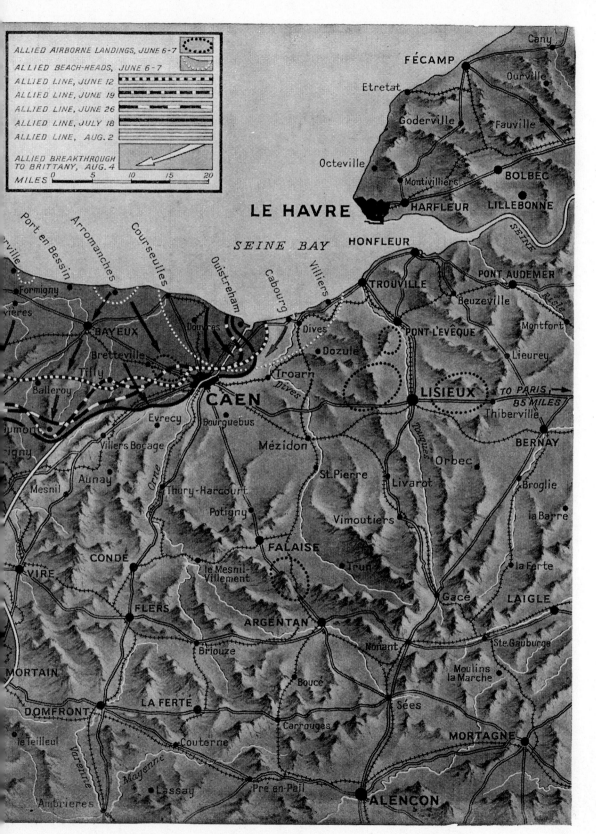

RUSSIANS ENTER VILNA. On 9 July, savage street fighting was in progress in the city of Vilna. The next day as many as 200 places round the city were occupied, so that it became completely surrounded. The enemy rushed airborne troops to reinforce the garrison, which barricaded itself into the centre of the city. The airport of Vilna was captured and its defenders completely annihilated. On 13 July, the capture of Vilna was saluted by 24 salvoes from 324 guns. The enemy dead amounted to 8,000 while 5,000 prisoners were captured. The booty

taken included 156 guns and 68 tanks. A statement by the German High Command admitted the loss of the city but claimed that the German Commander, together with the entire garrison, had fought his way out to the west. Similar and equally inaccurate claims had been made by the enemy after the fall of Vitebsk, Orsha, Mogilev, Bobruisk and several other strongholds along the northern part of the Eastern Front. The picture on these pages shows a self-propelled gun of the Red Army passing a disabled German gun in the shattered streets of Vilna.

U.S. LANDING ON SAIPAN. On 15 July,
American troops landed on Saipan Island,
a Japanese naval base in the Marianas

CAPTURE OF SAIPAN

On 12 and 13 June, U.S. battle-ships heavily bombarded Saipan. Heavy aerial bombing was also carried out by carrier-based aircraft upon the heavy defences of the island. The enemy lost 747 aeroplanes and 30 ships, while 51 others received damage in trying to repel the attacks. The Americans escaped with 4 ships damaged and 151 aeroplanes shot down. In the early morning of 15 July, U.S. assault troops went ashore. All heavy A.A. batteries had been knocked out by the preliminary bombing and shelling, and the landing force easily established beachheads and captured Agingan Point. The town of Charankanoa was captured on the same day and the Americans advanced inland in face of heavy fire, breaking up several Japanese counter-attacks. An official U.S. statement pointed out that as the Marianas were only 1,000 miles from Japan, the seizure of Saipan was an important step towards "bombing Tokyo." The island is the largest of the Marianas and was the seat of the government before the war. The picture shows American Marines digging in immediately after landing on the island.

R.A.F. BOMBS ENEMY ROCKET SITE

On 17 July, R.A.F. "Lancasters," "Halifaxes" and "Stirlings" carried out large-scale attacks on flying-bomb and long-range rocket sites. A large quantity of 12,000-lb. bombs were dropped, at least three of which scored direct hits doing immense damage. The whole of the cliff face round one rocket site collapsed, gravely affecting the main concrete structure. The tunnels leading to the underground workings were blocked, the whole railway system around was thrown out of gear and there was a general subsidence in all the neighbouring ground. A second visit was paid to this same site on 20 July when large gangs were found to be repairing the damage. In this raid, the main targets were the railway and machinery needed to bring up raw material for repair work and these were successfully dealt with. The photograph here was taken at a low level by a "Mosquito" on reconnaissance in the Pas de Calais. The figures indicate: (1) The concrete dome covering the underground workings. (2) Hundred-foot high crane which gives some idea of the size of the site. (3) A strong blockhouse completed. (4) A square concrete building in course of construction.

ADVANCE ON LVOV. On 23 July, the Russian offensive seriously imperilled the important German strong-holds at Dvinsk, Kaunas, Bialystok, Brest-Litovsk and Lvov. On this day, the town of Pskov, an important railway junction covering the roads to the southern regions of Estonia, was captured. On the following day, sixty inhabited places west of Pskov were occupied. Lvov was encircled on 26 July and a fierce battle was in progress to annihilate the enemy garrison. Next day, the city fell, an event of great importance, since not only is it a key-point

of the Ukraine and a political and economic centre, but also a large railway junction. It controls the trunk railways running through Silesia to Breslau and Berlin and the routes into Hungary and Czechoslovakia. It is only 200 miles south-east of Warsaw and therefore covers the way into Central Poland, and is 250 miles from Germany. Lvov was formerly the main German base in the South Russian front. The picture shows Russian artillery and tanks negotiating one of several river crossings while making their remarkable advance towards the city of Lvov.

CAPTURE OF BREST-LITOVSK

On 28 July, the Red Army captured Brest-Litovsk, an important railway junction covering the approaches to Warsaw. It had been occupied by the Germans for three years, and its strong fortifications had been completely restored. The German garrison had been ordered by Hitler to hold it at all costs. In the same area, sixty other places were also captured and west of the city Marshal Rokossovsky's troops encircled three enemy divisions which were being pushed back to the Western Bug and were in danger of being completely destroyed. By 29 July Marshal Rokossovsky was only twenty miles from Warsaw and the enemy rushed up reinforcements in an attempt to stop his advance. The same day, Praga, the industrial suburb of Warsaw, was under fire from Red Army artillery. Top, Soviet machine gunners advance through a town. Bottom, Russian self-propelled guns move through the streets of a liberated city.

ON THE EAST PRUSSIAN BORDER. On 30 July, General Chernyakovsky was advancing rapidly on East Prussia. His troops broke through the German defences on a seventy-mile front and advancing fifteen miles, captured 300 places. On 1 August, General Chernyakovsky captured the city fortress of Kovno covering the approaches to East Prussia. The enemy fought desperately to retain Kovno and in the street fighting the Germans lost 8,000 killed. By 3 August Generals Chernyakovsky and Zakharov had substantially broadened

their front in the drive towards the East Prussian border, from which they were now only a few miles distant. On 6 August, General Chernyakovsky crossed the Dubitsa River and fighting was taking place a few miles from East Prussia in the course of which thirty places were liberated. Key points behind the German lines were bombed by both the Red Air Force and the French "Normandie" Squadron. The picture shows Russian mobile guns passing horse-drawn supply wagons as they move into position along the frontier of East Prussia.

CAPTURE OF RENNES. In late July, the Americans began a drive into Brittany. By 2 August they were beyond Avranches, situated on the Norman-Breton border, and General Bradley was pushing on to Rennes and St. Malo. Rennes was reached on 3 August and all through the day there was a considerable amount of fighting in the streets. On the same afternoon other spearheads captured Dol and threatened St. Malo. On 4 August Rennes was completely cleared of the enemy by the Americans with the help of the Maquis working from inside the city. Photographs show the rejoicing. Top left, the inhabitants dance through the streets with American soldiers. Bottom left, American transports arrive in the centre of city. Above, French girls greet American soldiers.

FLORENCE CAPTURED. By 4 August, Allied troops were fast approaching Florence. The advance was badly hampered by demolitions but the New Zealanders captured Poggio dell' Monache, the last important obstacle. British troops drove up the Arno Valley and captured Rignano. The next day, the suburbs of Florence were in Allied hands. The South Africans, who first entered the city, received a tumultuous welcome from the inhabitants. The German communique stated that they had "withdrawn in the area north of Florence to spare the historic city and its irreplaceable art treasures." They had, however, previously directed artillery fire from the centre in violation of the declaration of Florence as an open city. The pictures show: above, Eighth Army troops in Florence; top right, Ponte Vecchio Bridge seen beyond a ruined crossing; bottom right, Florentines greet Allies.

GREAT RUSSIAN ADVANCES. During the summer of 1944 the Red Army made the greatest advances of the whole war. Thousands of square miles of Russian territory were cleared of the hated invaders. In the south the Red Army reached the important Rumanian oilfields and liberated Bucharest, the capital city. Deep advances were made into Poland, much of Lithuania and Latvia was set free, and the Russians reached Reich territory proper on the East Prussian frontier. The map on this page illustrates these remarkable Red Army achievements.

PROGRESS IN ITALY. Since the fall of Rome on 4 June, excellent progress was made northward through Italy by the armies fighting under the able command of General Alexander. The map reproduced above shows the important stages reached in the liberation of Italy in one year from the initial landings in the extreme south, or "toe," of the peninsula on 3 September, 1943. It also gives some idea of the mountainous nature of the country, which has made any accelerated or spectacular advances by the Fifth and Eighth Armies quite impossible.

ALLIED AIR FORCES OVER FRANCE. On 4 August, R.A.F. "Lancasters" bombed a rail bridge at Etaples and oil storage depots at Panillac and Bec d'Ambes, in addition to flying-bomb and rocket sites at L'Isle Adam, Trossy and the Pas-de-Calais. Rail yards at Montfort, Beauvais and Epernon were also attacked. An ammunition train near Bordeaux was destroyed and six bus loads of soldiers and four staff cars were blown up at Angers. Left, R.A.F. machines destroy a big oil storage depot behind the German lines. Above, an attack on enemy supply routes.

RUINED FRENCH TOWN. On 5 August, the Americans again advanced in several directions. One tank column reached Redon, while others pushed on in the direction of Brest and Lorient. Another pushed south-east and captured Fougères. By 6 August, the whole of the Brittany Peninsula was sealed off. The towns of Carbaix and Vannes were liberated with valuable aid from French Forces of the Interior. The German garrison at St. Malo rejected an ultimatum to surrender and continued to repel all attacks. By 7 August, the Americans were success-

fully closing in on Lorient and Brest. Great progress was made in the outskirts of St. Malo, where heavy fighting continued, and the following day the garrison surrendered after the capture of a disused quarry which they had strongly fortified. They had suffered enormous casualties and the tunnels in the quarry were found full of German dead. The enemy still continued to resist in Dinard, over the river from St. Malo, and in isolated points in St. Malo itself. The picture shows U.S. armour passing through the centre of a ruined town in north-western France.

ADVANCE ON FALAISE

By 13 August, the Germans were beginning to move large bodies of their infantry and tanks out of the Falaise gap but were leaving considerable forces within it which offered strong resistance to encircling Allies. British and Canadian artillery bombarded enemy escape routes east of Falaise. The following day, the Canadians launched a determined attack on a 4,000 yard front. Armoured troop carriers were used which moved forward under a dense smoke screen. Allied fighter bombers went ahead to destroy enemy strong positions. Between 2 p.m. and 3.45 p.m. over 700 R.A.F. "Lancasters" and "Halifaxes" dropped 4,000 tons of bombs on an area of only a few square miles which had been strongly fortified by the Germans. By evening, the Canadians had crossed the Laison river and were within a few miles of Falaise in spite of the fact that they had been bombed for nearly an hour by Allied machines owing to the similarity of their position to that of an enemy target. At nightfall, the Poles attached to the Canadians were engaged in savage hand to hand fighting with the enemy in the Quesnay woods. The picture shows the fires caused on Caen-Falaise road by bombing

ADVANCE IN NORMANDY. By 15 August, the Canadians had captured the high ground overlooking Falaise. Later in the day, they reached the outskirts of the town in spite of extensive demolitions and minefields. Meanwhile, the British by capturing Tinchebray and the Americans by capturing Domfront, and pushing on to Ranes, reduced the Falaise-Argentan gap to ten miles, with all the escape routes under Allied artillery fire. The enemy, however, managed to withdraw armour in faily good order in the direction of Lisieux by secondary roads. It was estimated, however, that 51,000 enemy troops remained in the gap, although the bulk of the German 7th Army was withdrawn. Left, prisoners pass through a Norman town. Above, a wrecked German convoy.

ALLIED LANDINGS
IN
SOUTHERN FRANCE

Throughout the night of 14-15 August the German system of coastal batteries and supply dumps on the coast of Southern France was deluged with thousands of tons of bombs. At dawn on 15 August, British and American paratroops were dropped behind the proposed landing beaches. Later those of the enemy batteries which had survived the bombing were mercilessly shelled from the sea by Allied battleships, cruisers, destroyers and rocket battery barges. At 8 a.m. assault craft, preceded by minesweepers and covered by an air umbrella, moved inland. The same day, the Allied Supreme Commander in the Mediterranean, General Sir Maitland Wilson, was able to announce that British, French and American troops strongly supported by Allied Air Forces were being landed on the south coast of France. In the evening, a communique announced that the landings were proceeding carefully according to schedule and were meeting with very little opposition. A supporting airborne operation was carried out successfully at the same time. Allied troops rapidly consolidated over a very considerable stretch of beach and throughout the day, fresh men and material were being landed without opposition. The picture shows a "duck" landing on the beachhead in the south of France.

FALAISE
CAPTURED

On 16 August, the Americans reached the outskirts of Falaise and the last remnant of the German garrison was cleared out after fierce fighting. On the following day, the town was firmly in Allied hands and the Falaise-Argentan gap was reduced to five miles. The entire civil population of Falaise, about 5,000 people, had fled. The medieval cathedral had been reduced to a heap of rubble and the whole town was in ruins. Meanwhile, the Allies pushed on in pursuit of the Germans. Important strongholds were captured at Vimont, Troarn, Barent and Mizidon. Polish troops pushed on to Trun, seven miles short of Argentan. Enemy resistance continued at Ranes. Top, Allied flame-throwing tanks in action (reproduced by permission of "Daily Herald"); below, the British and Canadians advance on Falaise.

ADVANCE CONTINUES. On 17 August the American Third Army was pressing on beyond Le Mans and Alençon with their wirelesses switched off so as not to indicate their position to the enemy. They liberated Dreux, Chartres, Chateaudun and Orleans and established bridgeheads over the rivers Eure and Aunay. Orleans fell with almost no opposition, and valuable aid was given by the Maquis in the capture of Chartres. They successfully prevented the Germans from destroying important installations and aided the Americans in gaining full control of the city. Although German snipers had used the Cathedral tower as a vantage point, the building was unharmed. Top left, Allied tanks near Caen. Bottom left, British tanks move into position. Above, Flers liberated.

ARGENTAN. On 20 August British troops entered Argentan, one of the last centres of resistance in the Falaise gap. A large part of the town was in ruins and blazing fiercely, shops had been pillaged and houses booby-trapped. By the close of the day the place was firmly in British hands. Above, the ruins of Argentan. The badly damaged tower of the fifteenth-century Gothic church of St. Germain can be seen in the background. Right, armour pushes forward in support of the infantry after the town has been made a ruin by Allied artillery fire. Some of the enemy still held out, but infantry followed up after the tanks and mopped up those who still resisted.

CLOSING OF FALAISE GAP. By 22 August the Falaise gap had been closed and mopping-up operations were in progress. The slaughter in the concentrated "killing ground" was very great and in the small village of St. Lambert the bodies of dead Germans and the wrecks of tanks and armoured vehicles choked the village street and the meadows round about. Very great numbers of prisoners were brought in, including Lieutenant-General Farmbacker and his entire staff. Meanwhile, the Allies continued to advance north and British forces took L'Aigle and Lisieux. In the advance, flying-bomb sites and a V.2 launching platform were seized. Left, Americans move over a hill-top in North France. Above, Americans clean up in a Normandy village.

233

ENEMY IN RETREAT. By 23 August the attempts to trap the German armies in the area bounded north by the Seine and south by Trouville, Lisieux, L'Aigle, Verneuil, Evreux and Vernon was almost achieved. Evreux and Vernon were captured and the village of Thiboutière was reached.   Heavy fighting was in progress in Lisieux, the Germans holding out desperately while they attempted to get as many men as possible across

the Seine between Vernon and the mouth. Every conceivable type of craft was used from rubber dinghies to large barges. Meanwhile, Allied guns pounded the evacuations in a twenty-mile "killing ground." The town of Lisieux was captured, although completely destroyed by the two-hour shelling which preceded the action. The picture shows American troops moving through a ruined town as they advanced to the Seine.

PARIS SEIZED. On 23 August a special communiqué was issued announcing the liberation of Paris. A general insurrection had taken place four days previously and 50,000 armed members of the F.F.I. together with several hundred thousand unarmed citizens took possession of the Ile de la Cité and held it against all German attacks. After four days' fighting the German attacks were repulsed everywhere, all public buildings had been occupied and Vichy representatives who had not fled were put under arrest. Top left, a tricolour on a captured German tank. Bottom left, flour being distributed in the city. Above, tanks lined up under the Arc de Triomphe.

ENEMY LOSSES IN PARIS

On 24 August an armistice was agreed upon between the citizens of Paris and the Germans in order to allow the latter to evacuate the city. The enemy had suffered very considerably in the severe fighting. A number of heavy tanks had been captured or destroyed and over 60 machine guns were taken. Some anti-tank guns and much equipment were among the booty and over 1,000 prisoners were taken. The Germans agreed to recognize the F.F.I. as belligerents. In the meantime, fighting went on at many points. In an action at one place, 400 patriots destroyed 10 tanks, 4 machine gun carriers, 21 lorries and 17 cars, besides inflicting considerable casualties on personnel. Top left, fighting before the Opera House. Bottom left, F.F.I. in action against German snipers. Right, prisoners from the German garrison being marched away.

PARIS LIBERATED. On 25 August, the French 2nd Armoured Division entered Paris. They were joined later by other Allied units and received a very warm welcome from the civil population. The Germans still held out at a few strong-points, including the Luxembourg Gardens, the Place de l'Etoile and the Place de la Republique.

During the rest of the day regular troops and civilians joined in a ferocious man-hunt through the Paris streets. By evening, enemy resistance was ended and General Scholtitz, commander of the German garrison in Paris, surrendered unconditionally.   Picture shows people falling flat in street as German snipers shoot at the crowd.

GENERAL DE GAULLE IN PARIS. After the capitulation of the German garrison, General de Gaulle arrived in Paris to celebrate its liberation from Nazi control

243

FRENCH TRAITORS EXECUTED. After the surrender of the Germans in Paris, all collaborators and members of the Vichy Government who did not succeed in escaping were placed under arrest and brought to trial. A number of French traitors—members of the Militia—had barricaded themselves in near the city area and had to be hunted out by patriots. The picture shows the execution of six young Frenchmen who had been members of the Militia and who were sentenced to death after having been found guilty of collaboration with the enemy.

This dramatic photograph was taken only a second or two after the shots had been fired and the smoke on the right was caused by the bullets hitting the wall after passing through the men's bodies. The Militia was a force created in 1940 by the Vichy Government to help the Germans and had been responsible for rounding up and killing many French patriots. The execution took place in the same square where a short time previously twenty-two French patriots had been executed by the Germans. French troops of the Interior composed the firing squad.

CROSSING THE SEINE. By 27 August, American and Canadian troops had crossed the River Seine in great strength at four points. Next day, the bridgehead was further widened and crossings were made at more points in the face of sporadic machine gun fire. On 29 August, bridgeheads on the Seine were again expanded, so that those at Louviers and Vernon were fused into one. The Paris-Rouen road was successfully cut and the Canadians came to within five miles of Rouen. Very rapid advances were made on 30 August and British tanks from the Vernon bridgehead covered thirty-three miles in twenty-four hours liberating Beauvais, Gournay and Marseille-en-Beauvaisis. Left, German prisoners. Above, General Montgomery crosses the Seine.

DIEPPE FREED
BY THE ALLIES

By 29 August, the German armies in North France appeared to be completely disorganized. The American First and Third Armies under Generals Hodges and Patton pushed on in the direction of the Belgian, German and Luxembourg frontiers. On 30 August, Rheims was taken by the Allies without any opposition. The city was almost untouched, and the Cathedral quite unharmed. The airfield outside the city was, however, very badly damaged as a result of Allied raids and seventy-five abandoned aircraft were taken. On the following day, American forces of the First Army were only ten miles from the Belgian border. The battle had turned into a rout and the enemy were fleeing so fast that it became difficult to keep in contact with them. Prisoners were being brought in at the rate of 2,000 a day and from sixty-four units. On 1 September, Verdun was taken with almost no opposition by the Third Army. Meanwhile the Canadian First Army had advanced along the coast where Dieppe was liberated without a shot being fired. The picture shows the ruined streets of the town after the Germans had left.

PARTISANS IN THE BALKANS. Throughout the spring and summer, Yugoslav troops were proving a great menace to Nazi troops passing through Slovenia into Hungary and very heavy casualties were being continually inflicted on the Germans. On 18 June, Marshal Tito's G.H.Q. reported that between 25 May and 10 June, the enemy had lost about 8,000 killed. On 19 June, the Yugoslav patriots opened a new offensive in Herzegovina which cleared the enemy from a large area. The picture shows Nazi troops filing over the Bosnian Mountains.

LIBERATION OF FRANCE. The map drawn by S. J. Turner, F.R.G.S., shows the limit of Allied advances up till 3 September. The Germans had been almost entirely expelled from Northern France although isolated garrisons at Havre and Brest still held out. In Southern France, almost half the area was liberated by the Maquis who had been doing work of supreme importance. In the early part of the year, they had been paralysing enemy railway and road traffic and interrupting telegraph and telephone communications, but later, occupied towns.

INTO BELGIUM. On 2 September, the British Second Army continued to advance rapidly north of the Somme. The Belgian border was crossed and lorry-borne infantry mopped up the small pockets of enemy resistance behind the spearhead of tanks. Lens, Douai, Bapaume and the famous Vimy Ridge (where the Canadian War Memorial was found undamaged) were all liberated. Meanwhile, on the coast, the 51st Highland Division, under Major-General Rennie, liberated St. Valery-en-Caux. Top left, tank loaded with infantrymen passes through a town. Bottom left, fifty-six German soldiers surrender to a single American soldier. Above, a snapshot found on a German prisoner showing some French patriots hanged in the main street of their own town.

ADVANCES IN THE PACIFIC. During the period 1943-1944 very steady and important progress was made against the enemy in the Far East, particularly in the Pacific area. By their successful and hard-fought campaigns in the Solomon Islands and New Guinea, the forces of the United Nations finally removed the direct threat of Japanese aggression to Australia. Had Australia, in fact, been invaded the main base of the Far East war would have been lost, and consequently it might have been prolonged indefinitely. Another certain result would have been an attack by the Japanese on the Pacific seaboard of the United States. How near the enemy did penetrate to the Australian mainland may be seen from the above map. Other important Allied gains were the clearing of Japanese forces from the Gilbert Islands and the Marshall Islands, which campaigns have been described and pictured on earlier pages of the present volume. With the opening of the campaign in the Mariana Islands and the

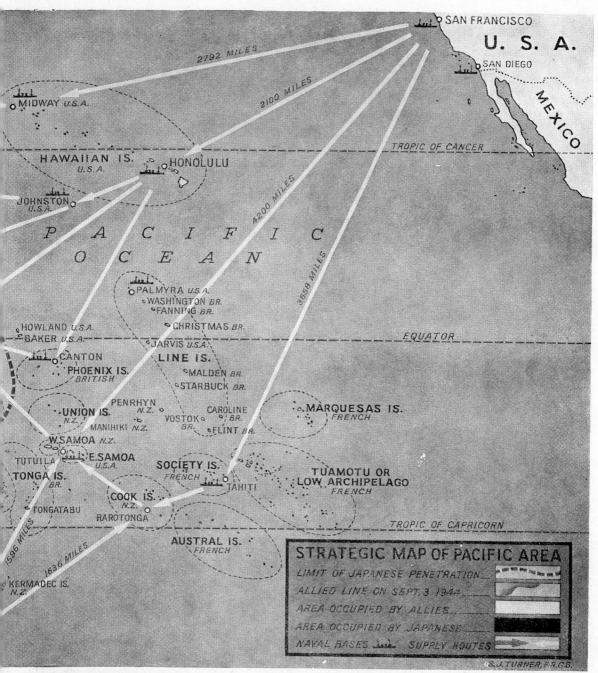

San Francisco · U.S.A. · San Diego · Mexico · 2792 MILES · 2100 MILES · 4200 MILES · 3658 MILES · MIDWAY *U.S.A.* · TROPIC OF CANCER · HAWAIIAN IS. *U.S.A.* · HONOLULU · JOHNSTON *U.S.A.* · PACIFIC OCEAN · PALMYRA *U.S.A.* · WASHINGTON *BR.* · FANNING *BR.* · HOWLAND *U.S.A.* · BAKER *U.S.A.* · CHRISTMAS *BR.* · EQUATOR · JARVIS *U.S.A.* · CANTON · LINE IS. · MALDEN *BR.* · PHOENIX IS. *BRITISH* · STARBUCK *BR.* · PENRHYN *N.Z.* · CAROLINE *BR.* · MARQUESAS IS. *FRENCH* · UNION IS. *N.Z.* · VOSTOK *BR.* · FLINT *BR.* · MANIHIKI *N.Z.* · W.SAMOA *N.Z.* · E.SAMOA *U.S.A.* · SOCIETY IS. *FRENCH* · TUAMOTU OR LOW ARCHIPELAGO *FRENCH* · TUTUILA · TAHITI · TONGA IS. *BR.* · COOK IS. *N.Z.* · TONGATABU · RAROTONGA · TROPIC OF CAPRICORN · AUSTRAL IS. *FRENCH* · 1596 MILES · 1636 MILES · KERMADEC IS. *N.Z.*

STRATEGIC MAP OF PACIFIC AREA

LIMIT OF JAPANESE PENETRATION
ALLIED LINE ON SEPT. 3. 1944
AREA OCCUPIED BY ALLIES
AREA OCCUPIED BY JAPANESE
NAVAL BASES   SUPPLY ROUTES

S.J.TURNER, F.R.G.S.

capture of Guam and Saipan, the war was brought much nearer to the homeland of the Japanese. Since the early part of 1943 the United Nations have built up a powerful navy and air force in the Far East and their strength is growing increasingly as every month goes by. Japanese losses both at sea and in the air have been heavy and damaging: on land, on sea and in the air serious inroads have been made into the enemy's manpower and material throughout the Pacific fighting areas. As the fourth year of war drew towards its close, the United Nations were on the eve of a great new offensive in the Philippine Islands. On 1 September U.S. planes made their first major bombing attack on the islands since the Japanese occupation. They dropped 111 tons of bombs on three airfields at Navao (Mindanao), destroying nearly forty Japanese bombers and fighters on the ground. The map above, specially drawn by S. J. Turner, F.R.G.S., shows the limit of Allied progress on 3 September, 1944.

THE AVENGING NATIONS WILL HURL THEMSELVES UPON THE FOE

"Britain . . . has never flinched or failed. And when the signal is given, the whole circle of avenging nations will hurl themselves upon the foe and batter out the life of the cruellest tyranny which has ever sought to bar the progress of mankind."

Extract from Prime Minister's speech of March 26, 1944.

Made and printed in Great Britain by Odhams (Watford) Ltd., Watford.   Copyright S.258.12R.AF.